A LITTLE MORE
CALM

A LITTLE MORE
PEACE

REFLECTIONS AND TOOLS
FOR CONSCIOUS LIVING

SEAN C. SULLIVAN

A LITTLE MORE CALM - A LITTLE MORE PEACE:
Reflections and Tools for Conscious Living

Published by Trinity Wellbeing Solutions
P.O. Box 258, Casino
New South Wales, Australia 2470
Email: info@trinitywellbeing.com.au
Website: www.trinitywellbeing.com.au

Book Layout ©2016 BookDesignTemplates.com

Cover Design by Trinity Wellbeing Solutions

Cover Photo: Wisanu Boonrawd/Shutterstock

A catalogue record for this book is available from the National Library of Australia

ISBN: 978-0-6482629-0-9

1. Self-help & Personal Development   2. Mind, Body, Spirit

Available from Amazon.com, CreateSpace.com and other online stores

This book is dedicated to Pachamama, our great Mother Earth and all her inhabitants.

And, particularly, to today's youth, who will inherit stewardship of our beautiful planet...

The Invitation

The reflections I have selected to incorporate in this book have unfolded over some 20 years of journeying. Along the way, I have experimented with many tools and processes, some successful and some not so, that have enabled me to, little by little, transform energy more effortlessly from states of restlessness to a state of peace.

I invite you unconditionally to be adventurous and courageous in your own path to self-mastery. It is every individual person's mission to discover the methods that resonate for them, that enable a transformation from the old restless consciousness, to a new awakened way of being in the world.

Vivid Dream

A strange land, a stranger time.
Faces unknown, my thoughts unwind.
Always searching, but never enough.
A race against time, calling my bluff.

Too much thought and contemplation, I have been told.
Can force a person to grow rapidly old.
But if we just sit a while, tranquil and relaxed.
The problems that we think we have can cease to exist.

So, open your eyes, my friend, seek and you shall know.
The mysteries that help sustain this super 3-D show.
And in the end, you'll see the truth, the light will set you free.
To the sudden realisation: It's all a vivid dream.

I sit alone in my special place and watch the world go by.
In search of that eternal question: Why? Why? Why?
When I ponder about the pain, the hurt, the memories and tears.
The conclusion's that these qualities are nothing but my fears.

So, I cease to feel, cease to see and let the pain pass by.
Though sometimes it is challenging to swallow my pride.
This superficiality is only in my mind.
But it's difficult to see this if your blind.

So, open your eyes, my friend, seek and you shall know.
The mysteries that help sustain this super 3-D show.
And in the end, you'll see the truth, the light will set you free.
To the sudden realisation: It's all a vivid dream.

I'll rise above the pessimism crushing me inside.
And watch the anger, pain and fear eventually subside.
I know that once I find my way, the pathway will be clear.
To further in this great pursuit of self-discovery.

So, open your eyes, my friend, seek and you shall know.
The mysteries that help sustain this super 3-D show.
And in the end, you'll see the truth, the light will set you free.
To the sudden realisation: It's all a vivid dream.

- Original Song Lyrics by Sean C. Sullivan

SEAN C. SULLIVAN

Contents

SEAN C. SULLIVAN

Preface

"So, when's the book coming out?" This simple question, posed to me by someone I had only just met, is probably how the journey of this creation all began. Towards the end of 2015, I attended a small wellness event in Tweed Heads, New South Wales, where I was exhibiting various wellbeing products and providing brief massage and energy medicine sessions. In one of the quieter moments, I happened to strike up a conversation with a spirit guide artist, and somehow the topic of Uluru came up. In that moment, I felt compelled to share some of the wisdom teachings that I had gratefully received during my visit to central Australia. Upon hearing about the insights that I had been gifted, the artist asked, in a rather suggestive tone, "So, when's the book coming out?" I smiled and replied, "Yeah, I guess I could give that a go".

Then, at the beginning of 2016, a potential opportunity arose to contribute to a collaborative book project. I submitted a piece of writing to my good friend and colleague in metaphysical teaching, for her review and feedback. Her comments about what I had written were so affirming, that I was again reminded of that same echoing, but encouraging, question: "So, when is the book coming out?" Within a couple of months, I had made the decision to dedicate a small amount of time every week to writing, and it was not long before I was being guided to write in a certain style, and I was even shown the number of key tools to include.

This was confirmed within weeks by a clairvoyant friend of the family, whose prophetic vision was yet another sign that I was destined to create an educational resource, based on my personal experiences and learnings. The whole process was enriching on a level that I had not experienced since my final year at university, when a student colleague and I were invited to co-author an article for the Queensland Journal of Music Education.

It was probably not until I had almost finalised the written manuscript, that the most intense realisation dawned upon me. Up until I began writing the Conclusion section of this book, I had been driven by an inner desire to share my experiences and learnings with others, who may, in turn, benefit from what I believed (and continue to advocate) are effective tools and insightful reflections. This is, indeed, still my objective; however, it suddenly became clear to me that I had written this book to remind myself of who *I* am. Wow! This was exactly the revelation that I needed to appear at that exact point in my life. Prior to that, I never realised that the person who may benefit the most from my book's contents would, in fact, be me!

I would love nothing more than for this book to act as an adjunct reference manual to a series of workshops and retreats that I intend to launch both online and in person. Many of the activities tend to peak in their potency in group scenarios, where the motivational energy moves on the level of the collective consciousness. Often, in my experience, if one person in a group is carrying a certain wounding or experiencing restlessness in one specific area of their life, there is an archetypal energy presenting that invariably resonates in some way with all in attendance. Similarly, when I first began writing, my goal was to make available an accessible avenue for people for whom attending a workshop may be either financially prohibitive, or energetically overwhelming. Although group energy can be incredibly powerful, the presented activities can certainly be undertaken by any individual person, anywhere, at any time, and do not require an expensive set of resources.

In all honesty, in the beginning I was not confident that I would be able to write an entire book; the demands of parenthood, in addition to working full-time, appeared to present obvious temporal limitations. I just knew that, if I achieved nothing else, I needed to pull out, and creatively express, what I had kept internalised for so long. I am incredibly thankful for, and humbled by, the wonderful opportunity I have now to connect with open-minded people for whom hopefully some, if not all, of my reflections and tools may have some significance or resonance. I warmly welcome your presence as we walk together along the road ahead, in search of a little more 'calm', a little more 'peace'.

Sean C. Sullivan

SEAN C. SULLIVAN

A LITTLE MORE

CALM

A LITTLE MORE

PEACE

REFLECTIONS AND TOOLS
FOR CONSCIOUS LIVING

SEAN C. SULLIVAN

SEAN C. SULLIVAN

CHAPTER 1

Introduction

Now more so than ever, I am deeply honoured and blessed to be here on this planet at this pivotal time in the evolution of Mother Earth and all her inhabitants. You see, I have an inner knowing that my whole life has been a continuous spiritual journey, in which I have danced from one profound experience to the next, being gradually and progressively guided to, and prepared for, this exact point in time. Over the past six years, I have dedicated much of my creative energy to exploring the nature of my essence as an energetic being, and to gathering reflections and tools that have nurtured, supported and facilitated a fundamental process of self-transformation.

I have worked with incredible shamans, musicians, clairvoyants and teachers, and have spent time in some amazingly sacred places. Even after what I consider to be numerous truly awe-inspiring and life-changing experiences over the course of my life, it was only very recently that I acknowledged my life purpose and, soon after, my soul's ultimate life path and destiny. As will become clearer as we share this time together, I propose a hypothesis that human beings ultimately share a common life purpose; what makes us individually unique is the way in which that life purpose is uniquely expressed or manifested, which can otherwise be understood as a 'life path'.

One evening at the beginning of 2016, my partner returned from a personal development workshop, and appeared somewhat deflated. I could sense in her energy that something significant was causing her a high level of concern. When I approached her about it, she commented that she had been told by one of her workshop mentors that there was 'still a bit of work to do'. For someone who had worked tirelessly over the previous four years shifting unwanted behavioural trends and self-limiting belief systems to find true value and meaning in life, understandably these words were somewhat disheartening.

As I engaged with the energy of 'a bit of work to do', I was overcome by an unexpected feeling of tranquillity; exactly how the next few simple words came in, I am not entirely certain, though they became my spiritual focus for the following several months and are the inspiration that underpins this creative project. I proceeded to say to my lovely partner in life: "No, darling...you do not have more *work* to do. You have more *peace* to find". My wife, Rachael, looked at me intensely, and I could see a noticeable change in her as she smiled, took in a deep breath and replied, "yeah, that makes much more sense". Two weeks later, I was blessed to have the opportunity to spend time with Peter Ramster, a clinical psychologist whom I consider to be one of the most knowledgeable past life regression therapists and dream analysts on the planet. Throughout one of his regression activities, the following words were repeated like a mantra, and have been etched in my memory ever since: "a little more peace - a little more calm". The notion of the importance of finding peace was certainly trying to get my attention!

So, I cannot really take credit for the title of this book; nor can I take complete credit for its contents. I have simply been a conduit for an expressive flow of universal energy and synergistic moments that have provided insight into my experience of life. As I have learned from the inspirational teachings of the Inca shamans, every gift we receive from the universe (Source, Spirit, God, however we each choose to refer to the energy of creation) comes with an obligation to share the wisdom of that gift with others. It has been rather intriguing the number of clients, colleagues, friends and family members with whom I have shared space in recent times who have expressed in some form or another that they are restless in one or more aspects of their lives. This has been yet another huge confirmation to me that every single human being, above all else, is searching for a sense of inner calm.

Self-development and spirituality are such broad and diverse fields. These days the various modalities, methodologies, ideologies, practices and techniques are so abundant in nature; it can be quite overwhelming when you are searching for information that both resonates and, is easy to comprehend. That was yet another influence underpinning my decision to make a dedicated contribution to the world of non-fiction literature. I wanted to strip back the labels associated with self-development and create an approach that was as simple as possible, particularly for people who are becoming curious about their personal growth and fulfilment and may be unsure about exactly where to look for guidance.

I was fortunate to have been raised in an accepting home environment in which the concept of spirituality was incredibly open and free from judgment. To this day, I remain confident that I was one of the most annoying students in classes that dealt with religious education. I was constantly challenging my teachers with counter arguments and alternative theories. Clearly, this was fuelled by an upbringing that encouraged a wider spectrum of possibilities than that which was achieved by subscribing to one single doctrine, or the limitations of a stand-alone faith system. That is not to say that each religious denomination or spiritual affiliation does not have wonderful insights to offer. After all, some of the most intriguing conversations I have ever had are with beautiful people who are dedicated to their chosen faith.

Into my adult life, I was blessed to be gifted an array of experiences and mentors that encouraged me to step beyond even the limitations of my own upbringing. A selection of these experiences I will share with you throughout the course of this book; others would be more appropriately postponed for a later literary project. What is important to note, is that I have attempted to present information that is both areligious and apolitical. Within my reflections are anecdotal examples from my own journey of Self, to illustrate the potency of some of the tools and processes available to everyone, that can facilitate the discovery of some of life's more peaceful moments and calmer states of being.

Essentially, the underpinning tenet of this book is the notion that a state of peace and calm is an attainable goal. The tools and processes detailed on the pages that follow, are by no means an exhaustive collection; they are but a selection of ingredients I have encountered that, when combined, can have incredibly powerful results. I have organised the latter chapters of this book in a deliberate way, to cover a sequence of movement away from resonance with what I term 'restlessness', to ultimately align more with a state of peace. To contextualise this more effectively, I have dedicated a brief section to examining the nature of stress and its evolution from prehistoric to contemporary times. Ultimately, to move from an operational model of stress and wounding to one of perpetual peace, I propose the following key ingredients:

1.   Identifying and naming the aspects of the Self that are restless;

2.   Balancing our internal masculine and feminine energetic polarities to enhance and maintain equilibrium in the mental, emotional and physical bodies;

3.   Taking some quiet, reflective 'alone' time to meditate and reconnect with both the Earth, and our inner world;

4.   Exploring the healing qualities and effects of sound vibration and music, and tapping in to that innate musical connectedness that resides within each of us;

5.   Discovering, nurturing and feeding your personal creative potentiality;

6.   Listening to, and becoming finely attuned to the subtle language of the physical body;

7.   Processing and releasing imbedded trauma, fear and underlying existing belief systems relating to the origins of feelings of restlessness, and re-programming our physical, mental-emotional and energetic systems with a new upgraded software package.

Every single person on the planet holds their own keys to wellbeing and wholeness. In my eyes, you, the reader, are already 'healed', already a complete version of yourself for where you are at this exact moment in time. I articulated this exact sentiment to a dear friend recently, who replied by asking me, "What do you mean? Are you saying that all the people who commit horrific atrocities in the world are perfect the way they are?" And I replied, "they are a perfect version of who they are for where they are up to in their soul's evolution, in this present moment". Originally, I had intended to defer my opinions about past lives until a later book; however, perhaps its relevance has appeared here.

Due to my own life experiences, I have reached the conclusion that we live many lifetimes. From what I have studied, witnessed and synthesised, as souls we choose to incarnate according to a set of predetermined guidelines, that we have already reviewed and agreed to, before we come in to this life. As I understand it, when our luminous form enters this three-dimensional reality, we agree to undertake certain roles, and to engage with specific experiences. In any one lifetime, some people will no doubt experience significant trauma or hardship, while others will appear to be born into relative abundance and never seem to want for anything. This is simply the illusion into which we are collectively inducted. My friend and colleague in metaphysical teaching, Leisa Sharp, once commented that she believed we are all here on this planet at this very moment in time, no matter the background from which we come, to simply "walk each other home". What a profound insight!

Perhaps you, the reader, have some energy to transform, or some trauma to explore; some wisdom teaching to uncover, or a just a little more peace to find. Wherever you are on your journey, I hold you sincerely and lovingly in the energy of infinite potentiality in this now moment, as we walk together through some simple self-focused processes that may (or may not) facilitate and enhance your own personal development. Just as every person on the planet is unique, so is their pathway to their inner divine. My unconditional hope is that, through sharing some of my personal reflections and engaging with some of the tools that I have found to be effective, you may bring a little more 'calm' and a little more 'peace' into your heart, and the hearts of all those with whom you connect throughout your journey of life.

Before discussing these tools in too much depth, I would like to begin by affirming my passion for the delivery of education to our youth, having spent time working in both formal and informal educational settings. My observation is that, although schools and individual teachers collectively have in their hearts the philosophy of nurturing the unique talents and abilities of every one of their students, the system appears to have, perhaps unintentionally, evolved educational curriculum into generic, quantitatively measurable, competitive, stress-inducing, labour force-driven programs. The first chapter focuses specifically on this topic, and offers a revised perspective on educational reform, suggesting that conventional curriculum must be underpinned by very specific qualitative outcomes.

CHAPTER 2

Separation to Integration:
A Revised Approach to Education

I t was a Saturday morning, and I had just taken a load of washing from the washing machine to hang on the clothesline. Incidentally, I had also just finished experiencing yet another one of my 4-year old son's aggressive tantrums, a behaviour that he would elicit rather manipulatively when he did not get his own way. Does this strike a chord with any parents out there? As I walked outside towards the clothesline, feeling a sense of inner frustration, I hoped that a small dose of nature and sunshine would alleviate my sudden disconnectedness to parental life.

I noticed that my neighbour was out in his back yard, playing with his two children. We exchanged pleasantries, and engaged in general neighbourly conversation, until one point when, for some reason, I commented: "You know, parenting presents the deepest wounds and the greatest gifts all in one package". Somehow, the experience of wounds and gifts in relation to parenting seems to resonate with many young mothers and fathers with whom I have spoken in recent times, and my neighbour was no exception. He replied, "yeah, I think all parents would identify with that". This very brief exchange provided enough insight for me to really reflect on my own experiences as a parent.

The Challenge of Parenting in a Time of Extremes

I will be completely candid at this point and say that I was totally unprepared for life as a father, and for the behavioural extremes with which I would be presented! I remember as a young parent pleading to friends and colleagues, "can you please turn to the chapter of that child-rearing self-help book that tells me what to do with *my* child?" The one key thing for which I was not at all prepared was the way children seem to know instinctively what buttons to push, and the best times to push them.

In truth, my children have been my greatest teachers. They regularly provide opportunities for me to look at how I carry energy. Children similarly enable the revelation that, as hard as we may try to be guides, mentors and models, we cannot control their behaviour any more than we can control the weather. My children do not belong to me; from my observations, parents are the conduits for enabling beautiful souls to experience a temporary human existence.

Unfortunately, due to our environmental programming, we tend to want to have control over every aspect of our lives, and our children are no exception to this. In one of my many deep conversations with my spiritual mentors, the notion of 'projection' was highlighted in relation to the way parents often offload to their kids. "It is amazing", one of my teachers commented, "how one day we can project so much of our own unresolved stuff on to the people we love the most, and next day they wake up, forgivingly, and just move on with life. Man!", he said, "now that is unconditional love at its most profound".

The most important point that needs to be made here, and it links into my discussions about the nature of education, is that, as parents, we need to ensure that our children have the practical and emotional skills available to not take on board the projections of others, be it family members, peers, teachers, or any significant others with whom they may interact in the course of daily life. This is particularly the case with young males, for whom the perceived societal limitations to what is an acceptable expression of certain emotions and feelings has no doubt contributed to the alarming prevalence of male youth suicide in Australia in recent years. Supporting our children to develop healthy ways of expressing themselves and providing specific tools and techniques for managing the potentially stressful challenges that life may present, would be perhaps one of the most progressive and fundamentally necessary focuses for educational curriculum in the 21st century.

When I first decided to organise my thoughts and experiences into a written format, my primary intention was to share a collection of reflections and tools that have progressively facilitated the process of my own journey from restlessness to inner calm and peace. My sincere hope was that my personal reflections, and the application of some, if not all the recommended activities, may in some way assist others in their own quest for purpose and meaning in life.

What I found along the way is that, ever since my departure from the world of teaching within a school-based context, I have become increasingly concerned with the education of (particularly) young people. My general impression is that the current model of education has become quite focused on, and driven by, quantitative measures and performance competitiveness. Teachers are now required to record and compile a phenomenal amount of information about every student's outcomes in relation to standardised benchmarks.

Unfortunately, from what I have observed, education professionals have, by default, become somewhat restricted in the way they deliver learning experiences, due to the demands of a systemic and politically-driven agenda, which has at its core the perpetuation of a skilled labour force that is motivated by 'making ends meet', ahead of making valuable contributions to a local and global community. The result is a growing population that is emotionally unbalanced, energetically disconnected, physically and psychologically unwell and heavily manipulated by the trends of social media and material satisfaction.

Based on that review, I feel it is my responsibility to dedicate at least a brief introductory portion of this book to proposing how the current education model would be richly enhanced by adopting a more holistic approach to curriculum, one which embraces individuality and emphasises the importance of the spiritual, rather than egotistical, evolution of humanity.

Spiritual versus Egotistical Evolution

Humanity has come a long way in the evolutionary cycle...or has it? Some would advocate that advancements in modern technology have paved the way for the industrialised world, but at what cost? We have fertilised and nurtured the collective human ego, perpetuating a scarcity consciousness, driven by fear of not having enough, and fear of not being good enough unless we conform to the latest fashion trend or get in the queue to buy the latest technological gadget. As a parent of a primary school-aged child, I enjoy reading the weekly school newsletters; they are often very informative. One of these articles, written by a Year 6 student, highlighted the significant detrimental impact that both technological devices and social media have on friendships, and generally the way in which young people interact.

The adult community has similarly been affected by mobile phones, computers and social media; in fact, in one of my university subjects (and we are talking over fifteen years ago now) we had to initiate online chat forums with classmates that were physically in the same room! Why not just talk to each other face-to-face? We have created ways to become close to people by physically distancing ourselves from them. An interesting concept!

As a society, we tend to retreat to our immediate family unit and go through our daily routine, somewhat disconnected to life beyond the four-walled safety of our homes, and our blinkered vision. How did things evolve that way? One theory that may contribute to our discovering a reason for such disconnectedness is that, as human beings we collectively lack an awareness of our divine nature. In feeding the ego, we have become heavily rooted in the physical and mental side of life, neglecting the very fact that we are energetic beings, born of the life-force energy of creation.

The Material Challenge and the Dilemma of Happiness

Further on, I will make some observations about how people define themselves and, more specifically, I note that success in the Western paradigm often appears to be heavily influenced by the accumulation of material possessions and monetary wealth, and the attainment of positional status on an occupational or academic hierarchy; in many respects, these tend to be the key performance indicators and measurements of the achievement of an individual, within both vocational and educational contexts. If we thoroughly deconstruct and examine this model, the reason that people can and do become so attached to tangible assets starts to become clear.

With the industrial revolution in the late 1700s came an increased global focus on mass manufacturing and commercial production, which simultaneously led to an increase in need for a skilled labour force, particularly in industries related to transportation, communication and finance. Over the subsequent 200-year period, the evolution of machinery and, more recently, technology, has created a seemingly sustainable market for products that would appear to enhance people's lives.

A perfect example of a company that revolutionised the technological stage would be Apple. Each year since the first iPhone was released on the market, Apple has upgraded its products and has catered itself directly to the demands of the consumer, to the extent that a number of people with whom I am acquainted, will line up to purchase the latest version of the Apple products, irrespective of the functional state of their superseded item. And so, it is with shoes, fashion, cars, televisions, and pretty much anything that consumers value. We have become a society that is dictated to by popular trends and driven by movements in commercial enterprise. Moreover, it would appear that we now go to work, not just to 'put food on the table' and 'pay the bills', but to support the continuity of a certain lifestyle, which has at its core a focus on having the latest fashion accessory, household item or technological gadget.

So, from where does this feeling of material worth really come and why does it affect us so significantly? To make things far simpler, let's firstly summarise the most fundamental contributing influences that may impact on our subscription to the belief system that success in life is all about what we do and how much we have:

∞   We have been born into a world that has progressively placed importance on the manufacture and distribution of machinery, clothing, technological devices, and other products and professional services that supposedly collectively enhance our lives and make us 'happy';

∞   From birth, we are educated (both formally and informally) that life (and our level of 'happiness') is about how much we know, what we can do with how much we know, and how much material wealth we can accumulate as a result of what we do and how much we know.

Based on this particular model, it is hardly surprising that people place importance on the accumulation of money and 'stuff', especially when a significant amount of time, effort and energy is invested in gathering it!

The notion of level of happiness in life is an interesting topic. There was a time when I believed that a person's level of happiness was a direct indicator of their success in life; however, as traditional Chinese philosophy demonstrates, to be continually happy is no more balanced than experiencing constant frustration. You see, happiness is an emotion, not a state of being, and it is healthy to experience a wide range of emotions, as they act as a guidance system that indicates where we are resonating, and whether we are in alignment with the messages of our soul. Through several key processes, human beings can learn how to use their emotional guidance system most effectively, while operating from an underlying foundation state of peace.

Wisdom from the Ancients

What would some of our wise and beloved ancestors say if they could share with us some of their observations about contemporary society? How is it that the evolution of the so-called 'civilised' world has become so driven by fear, conflict and competition? In traditional global cultures, the raising and teaching of children was a community responsibility, and education was considered the passing down of wisdom from one generation to the next. Before the conquistadors arrived off the shores of the Americas, the Incan elders intuitively knew that change was coming. The community that found safety and residence in the sacred Peruvian highlands maintained their culture and traditions without any outside interference for some 500 years after the arrival of the conquistadors.

Although their way of life may very well have continued to thrive even in the current global climate, the wisdom keepers of the twentieth century understood that the survival of their culture was dependent on the sharing of their knowledge with the Western world. It is not my purpose or intention to compare the past with the present; however, it is certainly worth examining particular aspects of the way of life some of our indigenous predecessors, in order to prompt further discussion as to how our current position could be improved.

Initiation and Rites of Passage

Within the ancient cultures of the world, the transition from childhood to adulthood was the shared responsibility of the elders of a community. During my visit to Uluru, which I will discuss in more depth as we continue, I heard how the men and women of the Ananu clan would mentor boys and girls who were coming into adulthood; the older male and female community members would share with the boys and girls (respectively) their dreamtime stories. They would impart the collective wisdom of the community so that each girl and boy inherited the knowledge of an entire community of experience. In all the traditional cultures, there were stages of initiation and rites of passage in which all

27

boys and girls were expected to participate, to be accepted as adults by the community.

In Western cultural traditions, it appears that most young people's initiation into adulthood is represented by a combination of the following key milestones: receiving a driver's licence, registering to vote, becoming inebriated for the first time, and losing one's virginity. Apparently (or so it would appear), none of these is underpinned by any common, agreed-upon, community-oriented ceremonial or educational philosophy.

During the editing stages of this chapter, it was pointed out to me by a close colleague and friend that secondary school graduation ceremonies are designed to symbolise and mark the achievement of a certain milestone; in some respects, this could be interpreted as a rite of passage for those who have achieved the completion of a high school education. Once again, please allow me to clarify that my comments are not intended to suggest that some educational institutions do not have initiations and rites of passage already embedded in their curriculum; however, based on my observations and research, such schools, like the one that I was fortunate to attend, are few, and tend to be rather progressive in their approach to instructional methodology.

During my educational studies, I undertook teaching practicum at an all-girls private school. One of the units of study that I was facilitating was entitled *Social Issues,* and was mainly concerned with information about HIV, AIDS and contraception. The students were intrigued about the topic but seemed somewhat lacking in knowledge for their age group. Based on my observations, I could deduce that some of the girls in the room were potentially sexually active and were extremely concerned about the information they had been hearing during the lesson. I questioned the girls about their impressions of the school's approach to sex education. I was surprised to hear that, in the opinion of these few senior students, who were not far off graduating from school, there was little guidance about sexual safety, neither from the school, nor from their parents!

With the nature of modern society and the way sex is exploited so liberally, this was a concerning revelation, to say the least. Why are sexual expression, intimacy and love such delicate topics, even in the current climate? After all, sex is the mechanism through which we all arrived here! Anyway, enough of the story...how can we, as a community of contributing adults, support our next younger generation more effectively? How do we equip our youth with the information they need to generate safe and effective relationships, with themselves, others and their natural environment? One theory suggests that the nature of relationships may require further attention if we are to fully understand and reorient the current situation.

Separation versus Integration

Somehow during the evolutionary cycle, as human beings we have changed the way we view ourselves in relation to one another and our environment. It would appear that we have become increasingly disconnected from a community-minded model of living, like the one with which the indigenous cultures of the world would be most familiar, instead aligning more with a way of life that has an everyone-for-themselves, competitive flavour. It is hard to pinpoint the precise reasons for this shift in consciousness, and though it would make an interesting study, it is probably more productive to concentrate on a solutions-oriented approach.

What I will propose emphatically is that we cannot continue to induct our youth into a world of separation, which has systematically resulted in conflict, competitiveness and environmental disconnectedness, while simultaneously hoping for, and anticipating, a reduction in anxiety, depression, substance abuse and youth suicide. Our entire educational model needs to be reviewed and reformed to reflect the attributes of *integration*. By very definition, integration is an act or instance of combining into an integral whole. We may admire, appreciate, accept and nurture an individual leaf for its uniqueness, while at the same time demonstrating an awareness that its existence is part of a greater whole - the branch, which can, similarly, be acknowledged for its beauty, must know too, that it survives as an extensive part of the tree. We can extend this ad infinitum to the ecosystem that supports the tree and beyond.

Figure 1: The anatomy of a leaf

Looking at the anatomy of a leaf, as pictured in Figure 1, we can observe that its skeletal structure represents a miniature version of an entire tree. Education can be viewed in a similar way. At the macro level, educational reform must have as its primary tenet, how as a global community, we want our next generation to *be*, rather than what we want them individually to *know* or be able to *do*; this must then be reflected at a community and institutional level. Teachings, such as those embedded within the Inca shamanic Medicine Wheel training, would be highly effective tools to pass on to our younger generation, so that they are empowered with key techniques to help them move through life in a more connected way; to enable in them the skills to live consciously, and address trauma when it occurs without accumulating compounded wounding that will require more in-depth intervention at a later stage in life.

It is comforting to know that there are dedicated authors and educators who have already proposed, and are continuing to generate, more holistic and interconnected discussions around school-based education. Numerous highly-respected spiritual teachers have spoken passionately about the need for a global shift from the default way in which children in Western society have been, and continue to be, inducted into the world.

Typically, human beings start out innocently in the world as fun-loving children and gradually develop into young adults conditioned with a career-focused ideology, which is the fabric upon which we then tend to base most of our existence. This model imposes that life, and in fact our individual identity, is determined by how much money we can make, how many worldly possessions we can acquire, to what extent we can climb the social and occupational hierarchy, how much better we are than the next person, and finally to what extent we are approved of, and accepted as valid people, by others in our environment.

By now, I have no doubt set the tone for the next chapter, in which we will delve, albeit somewhat superficially, into the nature of stress and its historical evolution. I will conclude this section by proposing that, collectively as human beings, we need to make a shift in consciousness from the 'having' and 'doing' model of living to a more purpose-driven, self-actualising approach. With the expression of 'purpose' rather than 'career' as the driving force, we can live a life of dharma, following our individual life pathway, the success of which is no longer measured by wealth, occupations, or the opinions of others, but by our level of personal contentment, connectedness and contribution to the circle of life. There are some key teachers and spiritual leaders who have already spoken similarly about the urgent need for a collective shift in consciousness. I look forward to sharing future conversations, revelations and reforms that result from networking with others, so that the education of our next generation inspires a more balanced, environmentally-connected, and spiritually-enriching outcome.

CHAPTER 3

The Evolution of Stress: From the Saber Tooth Tiger to Modern Lifestyle

Stress has become an increasingly concerning part of our daily lives. It appears that, in almost every aspect of the human experience, there exists the potential for some manner of stress-inducing stimulus. It is so impactful, that medical professionals often refer to particularly psychological stress, as a key factor that determines our overall wellbeing. Based on my interactions with colleagues, clients, family and friends, and from general societal observations, there are three themes that I have identified as contributing significantly to most of the population's personal stress: Financial position, stability of personal relationships and health.

But what *is* stress and how does the body process it? Have human beings always experienced it, and has the nature of our relationship with stress evolved over time? I am certainly not the first person to raise such thought-provoking questions; health professionals have been investigating the nature of stress for decades. In my personal experience, there are typically three different forms of stress that affect human beings, each of which I will elaborate on as we move forward:

1) **Physical stress**, experienced in response to a definitive threat to our safety or survival;

2) **Trauma-induced stress**, which is triggered by the memory of a real physical, emotional, mental or energetic wounding that has occurred in a person's life, and has left an imprint (this can be conscious, or may be buried deeply within the unconscious); and,

3) **Psychosomatic stress**, which is neither a response to survival, nor related to trauma, but is a by-product of a growing societal ideology that is underpinned by both fear, and quantitative or qualitative competitiveness.

Both physical and trauma-induced stress are the result of real environmental causes; psychosomatic stress, however, is based on perceived rather than actual threats, a state of mind into which people tend to talk themselves and is most likely the primary factor contributing to a growing global fear mentality. As will unfold, I propose the hypothesis that, the significance and intensity of stress has dramatically shifted over time, from its innate function in traditional cultures as a tool for survival, to nowadays a common way that humans function every day – a behaviour that is perpetuated by the increasing demands of the human ego. To both understand the nature of stress more intimately, and to contextualise its role and manifestation in contemporary times, I would firstly like to delve into both the basic biology of stress, and the role of physical stress in prehistoric times.

Human Physiology and the Saber-Tooth Tiger

In almost every first-aid, kinesiology or other wellbeing workshop I have ever attended, reference has been made to the fight-flight-freeze response; the physiological message that begins in the limbic brain, which sends signals to the hypothalamus and pituitary gland, triggering the release of specific hormones that signal the adrenal glands, resulting in the secretion of the neurotransmitters epinephrine (or adrenaline), and cortisol. This is, of course, an incredibly simplified description, and prior to studying anatomy and physiology, I really had no idea about the intricacies of the human body!

The process of preparation for the ultimate decision to either flee from a predator, or stay and fight, is undoubtedly an in-built, evolutionary mechanism for physical survival. Although there is a generic outcome when adjusting to potentially life-threatening situations, the curious element is that each individual person responds to potentially stressful circumstances in different and unique ways. The same neurotransmitters – epinephrine and cortisol – are released in situations that tend to create a high-level of excitement, such as extreme sporting activities; in this case, the 'rush' of adrenaline seems to enable thrill seekers to carry out potentially life-threatening actions, with limited (if any) concern for their survival.

Contrasts have often been illustrated regarding the nature of modern-day stress when positioned against historical patterns. I have heard many times that "we are no longer running away from saber-tooth tiger". For obvious reasons, I started to believe that the saber-tooth tiger preyed on *Homo sapiens*, and I became intrigued by this animal's influence on the human psyche even some 10,000 years after its extinction. Based on my own investigations, it is highly improbable that human beings were ever on the saber-tooth tiger's dinner menu! It appears that after all this time, we may very well have misunderstood the saber-tooth tiger's intentions. From what I understand, although saber-tooth tigers were carnivorous, they preyed upon herbivores, perhaps because they were intuitively aware of the nutritional benefits of eating herbivorous creatures.

What is probably most crucial to point out here, is that both early human beings and the saber-tooth tiger were drawn to similar food sources. We do know that it is possible that humans were killed by the saber-tooth tiger, and in all honesty, the saber-tooth tiger probably was a real threat to human survival; our ancestors were no doubt wise to avoid confrontation. One could draw the conclusion at this point, however, that the saber-tooth tiger and our caveman friends were more like rivals, competing for the same prize.

Seriously, in 10,000 years, how much about *Homo sapiens* has really changed? People continue to be driven by competition, success and victory; the difference is that what we are competing for is no longer determined solely by our physical survival needs. What is similarly concerning is that, when secreted in too high quantities, too frequently, our body's natural stress-management pharmaceuticals can become dangerously toxic. I would go one step further, and suggest that some illnesses and diseases are, in fact, by-products of the way some people choose to 'do' life.

Stress and Spirituality

Before I fully understood my deeper spiritual calling, and decided to embark on my shamanic apprenticeship, one of my mentors remarked, rather candidly, "the shamanic path is not for the feint-hearted". She continued, "once you start on this journey, there is no turning back". I heard these words very clearly, and I have always accepted the challenges of life with an open heart; after all, exploring spirituality at a much deeper level sounded like such a rewarding endeavour. I never really anticipated that, in striving to pursue a more fulfilling, spiritually-aligned life, I would simultaneously experience significant inner turmoil and potential upheaval; I mean, it seemed almost counter-intuitive! Over a period of time, I was to discover that the more we grow and feed our luminosity, the broader our shadow becomes. When I finally made this realisation conscious, I could see that light and dark were simply two extreme ends of a continuously expanding spectrum, and that the secret to finding a state of peace was to position myself in the centre of the continuum.

Not only was I searching inwardly to find balance between my light and shadow aspects, but there was also a yearning to find a sense of purposefulness in my life; ironically, I have encountered a number of people on a spiritual pathway for whom discovering purposefulness competes much more prominently for their attention than any other potentially stressful stimulus. So powerful is the notion of fulfilling a life purpose, or following a certain life path, that for some people, purposeful living can become an obsession or fixation, which detracts somewhat from the concept of 'conscious living', which will be discussed further as we continue. Consider the following authentic scenario.

Bernadette is a young mother of two school-aged children. Earlier in her life, Bernadette worked to become academically skilled, and gained employment in her chosen field upon graduation from university. She was raised in a competitive environment in which academic and financial achievement was a measurement of success. As a mature adult, she felt that something was missing in her life. More succinctly, she was restless about who she was as a person, and her situation in life; she felt neither inspired nor fulfilled and longed to understand her soul's unique expression. Bernadette readily attended courses in personal development, hoping that by doing so she would, in synchronicity, discover the greater meaning and purpose behind her existence. Given that she was particularly literal in her approach to life, Bernadette often had difficulty seeing the mythical signs and symbols that presented to her in her daily activities. Bernadette's significant time investment in her own growth and development, and her continuing search and yearning for meaningful experiences, eventually resulted in considerable frustration and, ultimately, a high level of stress.

Conscious living, the idea of being aware and present in every moment, is a theme that is no doubt familiar, particularly to those who have subscribed to the wonderful contributions of some of the great spiritual influences of our era. One of the most consistent observations made by modern-day spiritual teachers is the notion that by very description, as humans our experience is about 'being' and not about 'doing'. This ideology of self-definition according to 'doing' is further fuelled by a growing global fear mentality. Let us examine this in a little more depth.

The Nature of F.E.A.R.

It is 4:00am on a Wednesday morning when all I really want to do is catch up on some long-needed rest! But the message I receive is so persistent, that I am wide awake, upright in bed and have no choice but to interpret the incoming energy. Have you heard one of the popular acronyms for the word F.E.A.R.? It is False Evidence Appearing Real. Much of what builds stress and anxiety in current times is borne out of the illusion that somehow the car you drive, the job you have, the house in which you live and the clothes you wear, are indications of your achievements in life. This is the underlying essence of what I have referred to as psychosomatic stress.

It is important to acknowledge that our endocrine system is often working overtime to process False Evidence, rather than actual threats to our survival. In the year 1999, a noticeable percentage of the population was so convinced that the so-called 'millennium bug' would strike, that they stocked up on candles, tinned foods and other supplies, and built bunkers underground in case their worst fears were to eventuate. Of course, this was probably never likely to happen – nonetheless, the false belief system they held was so powerful that it became their truth.

During my shamanic apprenticeship, I was required to visit the aspects of myself that held the energy of fear, for it is fear that inhibits the flow of trust in the life process. One of the biggest fears with which I was presented, was my fear of failure. In my final year of university, and all through my teaching life, I held onto a high-achieving belief that I had to get top results; any mistakes or signs of imperfection I would take very seriously, as they represented a self-diagnosed deficit in my professional character. It was to become clear that my obsession with perfectionism was related to a need to be seen by others as intelligent. I had to shift the False Evidence, the part of myself that was constantly looking to others for approval, to allow space for self-acceptance and an unconditional love of my true essence.

It is amazing how early in life we start to define ourselves by our external world, constantly seeking validation from others as to our worth. I was observing my 5-year old son and 7-year old daughter playing a card game called *Memory*. In this game, all the cards are laid out randomly in a face-down position. The way the game is played is by turning one card up, followed by a second card, which hopefully matches the first card to form a pair. My two children are so competitive – at the end of the game they count the number of pairs, both excited about the prospect that they have 'won' the most pairs. My son counts out 11 pairs, while my daughter counts 14. You can just feel the air thicken as my son reacts forcefully by exclaiming "but I wanted to win!"

A part of me is silently perplexed about what I am witnessing, while another part suddenly blurts out with conviction "but what is it that you are trying to win? What are you possibly going to gain by beating your sister?" Both kids stare at me blankly, as if I had grown a second head. I turn to my daughter and ask, "so do you just want to get the most pairs to be better than your brother?" And now comes the interesting part: My daughter just nods her head softly and looks at me as if to say "well, yeah Dad…what else would we play this game for?" And in that moment, it was made abundantly clear that somehow, my kids had learned the importance of winning at all costs.

I started to look retrospectively at how I had raised my children, thinking that somehow, I had a role to play in shaping this competitive behaviour. I was considering the notion of lineage, and the possibility that their competitiveness was genetically, or energetically, linked to my own, earlier fears, when my son then asked, in an almost emotionless and rehearsed tone, "Dad…can I turn the TV on?" It does appear that in modern times, the television is a popular way of escaping our stressful reality. I admit it may be a way of relaxing and disconnecting from the events of the day. It is somewhat concerning though, given that television tends to be one of the most influential forces perpetuating loaded social attitudes and popular cultural trends, which often model False Evidence. Moreover, the act of watching TV of an evening is not actively addressing or resolving the day's stressful stimulus; it is a passive distraction. In the morning, the cause for yesterday's stress will probably present again, and will likely result in a similar outcome.

Thankfully, as I have emphasised, there are tools and strategies available that are simple to undertake and easy to apply to our daily routine, so that we can begin to move through stressful circumstances proactively and transform the energy of stress into a useful ally. We can develop the insight to change financial constraint into financial liberation; we can shift our awareness from psychosomatic illness to psychosomatic wellness; and we can transform the memory of painful trauma into a wisdom teaching or gift.

CHAPTER 4

A Little More Peace
and Conscious Living

To truly know the way of peace we must visit all the aspects of the Self that are restless. I will elaborate more on this idea of restlessness in Chapter Nine, when we look in more depth at the nature of trauma and wounding. I will propose at this point that it requires a significant quantity of life force energy to fuel and maintain heightened states of fear, toxic emotion, physical stress and mental eruptions. On the other hand, operating from a place of balance, trust and peace is far less consuming; in fact, it is energising.

As we continue, I will present a collection of my own reflections and some practical self-guided processes that I have gathered over the past few years, which have enabled me to bring a little more 'calm' and 'peace' to both my internal and external worlds. Some of these have been shared with me throughout my Inca shamanic training and various personal development experiences; others are beautifully simple, yet profoundly effective gifts from the universe that I have received in my own personal spiritual practice.

Truthfully, my primary objective in this reflective process is to activate the light quotient at the atomic level of each individual cell in every person who reads these words, to its pure potentiality to self-transform. I continually observe the way in which human beings project their desires, expectations and responsibilities onto others in the benign hope that someone or something external to themselves will somehow be able to 'fix' their circumstances, fill an inner void, or correct their supposed deficiencies. That said, I have certainly witnessed the reverent ways in which practitioners of shamanic energy medicine hold an individual client, and even an auditorium filled with workshop delegates, in a powerfully loving, healing and transformational space.

Ultimately, it is every individual's mission to take ownership of the relationships they form with both themselves and their external world. This is the essence of living consciously. Conscious living is having an explicit awareness that, in every moment, we make choices about how we engage with the world; it is releasing oneself from past traumas and feelings of regret for missed opportunities. Similarly, it is not fearing what the future may or may not reveal. It is embracing every potentiality in the present moment and making the most of every breath.

Living Consciously

Conscious living requires us to be introspective, to ask ourselves questions about why we do things the way we do. If I observe my own behaviour, and I blindly accept something that I do automatically because it's the way I've always done it, or it's the way my parents did it, then I am not really looking closely at my decision to continue doing it. One of my observations made when I was working in an administrative office was the number of sales reports that were printed out every day. At one point, I asked the question "what do we use these reports for?" The response I received was "I'm not really sure, but we have always printed them out". Personally, I could see no purpose or benefit in wasting time and resources printing a report that nobody ever looked at, just because it was item number 4 on the list of things to do in a routine work function.

Admittedly, many people do tend to subscribe to the 'creatures of habit' perspective. Based on what I have seen and supported by the work of many colleagues in the personal development field, human beings appear to have an in-built default software program that determines our likely behaviour and the way in which we will probably express our personality in any given situation. This default program can determine our reactions to life challenges, the way we interact with people, how we solve problems that arise and generally how we express ourselves in the world.

The software is made up of our personal life experiences, including triumphs and traumas, and our lineage - the DNA we inherited from our parents. Many people (me included) would advocate that karma and past life experiences also have significant roles to play in how we 'do life'.

So how do we upgrade our software? Exactly how do we 'do life' better? Well, it is a progressive and strategic process. Firstly, we need to identify certain behavioural patterns or personality trends that do not really serve our highest good. In other words, we must name all the parts of ourselves that are restless. Secondly, we need to hold a vision in our hearts of what we desire instead. Most importantly, we need to recognise that upgrading software is not an instantaneous process. Those of you with iPhones will appreciate that sometimes the App Store prompts you to update a number of Apps. The first time I saw that there were 15 Apps that needed updating, I figured that I could update them all at the same time. Things did not really work out the way I had anticipated and the screen on my iPhone froze. I had asked it to change too much all at once. The next time I updated several Apps, I decided to select one App at a time and upgrade the software individually. This was a far more advantageous approach.

Rachael and I recently looked around us at home and we both felt that there was a huge quantity of unwanted clutter in almost every room of our house. She looked at me and asked with a solemn face "how are we ever going to clean up all this stuff?" I replied, "one room at a time, darling". You see, if we look at ourselves as an entire house, similarly we are likely to encounter an overwhelming number of things that might need to be altered in order for us to live blissful lives. If we simply focus our energy on one aspect at a time and get that one aspect working to our satisfaction, we would find de-cluttering ourselves, and upgrading our software, a very simple and rewarding process.

Activity 1: Visiting the Parts of the Self that are Restless

Part 1

I invite you now to reflect deeply and creatively on the parts of yourself that are restless. Having a dedicated journal or notebook for these activities is ideal, as you may be interested to look back over your collective reflections at a later stage. It is recommended to follow this process step by step, the reason for which will become apparent as we move forward.

The first time I engaged with this activity, I started by making a note of all the aspects of my life with which I was not totally content, or not in right relationship (the term 'right relationship' is often used in shamanic work to denote the universal energy of exchange – the balance between giving and receiving. We will talk about this concept in more detail in Chapter 5). For example, I started with a list which contained general areas of my life, like:

- ∞ Work life and Career
- ∞ Health and wellbeing
- ∞ Love life
- ∞ Friendships
- ∞ Family
- ∞ Financial stability
- ∞ Hobbies and Leisure
- ∞ Etc.

This is purely an example to get you started. Take some time to explore your own circumstances – you may find many more areas than those detailed above. Remember, this is a very personal list, which no-one else needs to view.

Part 2

Review the list that you have created. See if there are any common themes that appear. Can you group the aspects of your life into main categories? For example, I have listed 'love life', 'children' and 'work colleagues', so have chosen to call my first category 'relationships with other people'. The idea is to come up with 5 or so main categories. Leave some space between each category you come up with so that you can reflect further on each.

You can now really strip back these aspects and examine exactly where you are resonating in relation to each area. Look at the first category you have written, become aware of 'how' you are when you read it. Remember, this is an aspect of your experience of life that triggers a feeling of restlessness; in other words, you are not totally at peace in relation to this area of your life. What feelings come up for you around this? In my example of relationships with others, I noted feelings like 'control', 'judgment', and 'self-worth'.

For each category, try to note at least 3 observations or feelings that come up for you. You may also note any physiological feelings that you observe. Does your body feel tense anywhere when you focus on any of these feelings? Any information, however trivial or minor it may appear, is crucial to pinpoint, as it will provide a solid foundation for our further discussions, and a subsequent activity in Chapter Nine that looks at the nature of trauma and wounding.

Comments / Notes / Observations

CHAPTER 5

Balance and the Law
of Sacred Exchange

'In Balance We Grow'. These four words constituted the motto of the secondary school I attended some 25 years ago. Back then, and probably until relatively recently, I understood balance primarily as it relates to lifestyle. I have lost count of the number of times I embarked on a New Year reassuring myself and others of my desire to spend less time at work and more time with family; to exercise more, or to have a more eventful social calendar. While having a balanced lifestyle is indeed an important ingredient in maintaining good physical, mental, emotional and energetic health, there are other ways in which balance plays a crucial role in our wellbeing. There are three specific revelations regarding balance that I felt compelled to share, which have impacted significantly on my work with Self and others. Firstly, I invite you to journey with me back in time to May 2015, to the heart of the Earth Mother: Uluru.

The Eight Aspects of Feminine-Masculine

Standing next to the Rock is a somewhat humbling experience. Like most pilgrimages and vision quests, it was to become clear that the reason I thought I had come to this incredibly powerful and sacred place, was not, in fact, the purpose of my mission here. I was travelling with a small group of beautiful healers and light-workers who all felt the magnetic attraction of Uluru. To be honest, I believed that I had embarked on a voyage with the objective of undertaking profound planetary work. Now, I intend absolutely no disrespect to my colleagues and travelling companions, nor to all the wonderful spiritual and shamanic mentors and healers with whom I have had the utmost pleasure and honour to work; however, I can honestly say, without equivocation, that the most significant and profound transformational experience that I have had to date, was a one-on-one journey with the Rock. Allow me to elaborate.

For quite some time, I had experienced a sense of discomfort whenever I held my partner's hand. For some reason, whenever my hand was held an aspect of me wanted to pull away or retreat to my own personal bubble. It had become apparent to me that some part of me was not in right relationship, was not in balance. Upon further reflection, it was revealed that the apprehension was experienced predominantly on one side of the body. This was intriguing. My colleagues were tracking a possible past-life link that may require shamanic intervention, either through *soul retrieval* or *extraction* (*soul retrieval* and *extraction* are energy medicine practices learned during the Inca shamanic apprenticeship, known more generically as the *Medicine Wheel*); given our proximity to Uluru, it was also suggested that this imbalance had presented for a pivotal reason!

During a morning meditation, I was shown very clearly to connect and journey directly with Uluru for further guidance, and that two stones in my *mesa* (shamanic medicine kit) would facilitate the process. Specifically, I was guided to walk around the base of the Rock in an anticlockwise direction, holding my sacred masculine and feminine calibration stones – one in each hand – for the duration of the circuit. Every now and then, I would be prompted to interchange the two stones between my left and right hands. When I questioned the purpose behind this, I was swiftly told (perhaps by my higher Self) that the wisdom teaching would come when I fully trusted and opened myself to the potential transformation that could occur by undertaking this three-and-a-half hour-long trek. With stones in hand, and some two hundred or so flies as my travelling companions, I opened *sacred space* (we will discuss this process in Chapter 9) and set off around the base walk.

At various times on the circuit, I was guided to pause and reflect, to ceremony, to commune with the ancestors, and connect my stones directly with the heart of the Earth Mother. I could share numerous stories about my encounters on this brief journey; however, these are probably for another time. Suffice it to say that, as I neared my approach to the conclusion of the circuit, I was inundated with a cognisant and sentient knowing, a wisdom teaching that I did not anticipate, and had never even considered until that moment. Without looking down at my hands, I now had no idea which stone was in which hand. Somehow, it now all made sense; I had just received my most amazing and transcendental transmission of celestial wisdom.

The masculine-feminine relationship had always been very present with me; not only had I studied the nature of duality in my shamanic journeying, but I had also formally studied oriental philosophy and was well-versed in the role of the Yin-Yang theory within the historical context of oriental medicine. What I did not know until now, is that the divine feminine - sacred masculine interplay within the human energy field has eight aspects. I could understand more clearly now the possible underlying reasons why, so many people find balance such a challenging state of being to achieve. These eight aspects influence our relationships with people, our life experiences and the way in which we carry energy in relation to traumas, challenges, obstacles and wounds. "So, what are these eight aspects?", I hear you ask, "and how do they play out?". Well, I will attempt to be as succinct as possible.

In many traditional models of energy medicine, the right side of the body has been depicted as holding the masculine, or 'giving' role and the left side the feminine, or 'receiving' role. In fact, this understanding had underpinned the very nature of my own energetic medicine practices up to this point. Instantaneously, I knew in my entire being what I now share with you:

1. The Divine Feminine receives from the Divine Feminine;
2. The Divine Feminine receives from the Sacred Masculine;
3. The Divine Feminine gives to the Divine Feminine;
4. The Devine Feminine gives to the Sacred Masculine;

5. The Sacred Masculine receives from the Sacred Masculine;
6. The Sacred Masculine receives from the Divine Feminine;
7. The Sacred Masculine gives to the Sacred Masculine; and
8. The Sacred Masculine gives to the Divine Feminine.

In any given moment, one or more of these eight pathways can be out of right relationship. Through basic muscle testing, the nature and location of imbalance can be easily detected and much more effectively processed. Just consider for a moment one aspect of your life that has presented an obstacle or challenge; now examine the relationship between you and the challenge or obstacle. Are you giving unconditionally and receiving gracefully? Is it the masculine or feminine aspect that is doing the giving and/or receiving?

Put very simply, when the 8 aspects are in perfect synergy, the central energetic pathways move like the DNA double helix, the cellular genetic building blocks of all human life forms. When our feminine and masculine energies are totally balanced, and aligned, they move effortlessly along the body's central channel, enveloping the seven chakras, in much the same way as the caduceus, or kundalini resonance. Once mastered, this frequency is a powerful key to achieving physical, mental, emotional and energetic balance in just about every dimension of your life. I would like to expand this notion of balance a little further and delve into some of the knowledge and practices of the Inca.

Ayni, the Shadow Self and Sacred Exchange

Within all traditional Indigenous cultures, there was a deep understanding of the sacred relationship between people and the Earth. Mother Gaia nurtures, grows and provides; in return, people made ceremonial and sometimes sacrificial offerings in exchange. Ancient Peruvian wisdom teachings consistently refer to a principle known as 'right relationship' or 'sacred exchange'. Fundamentally, when humans interact in any exchange, they are giving and receiving *ayni*, which is the Quechua word used to describe the life force energy that moves through, and interconnects, all things. The more balanced our reciprocal flow of *ayni* in our actions of giving and receiving, the more aligned we are with each other, with nature and with the Source of all creation.

Consider how frequently you offer an affirmation of gratitude for the wonderful gifts you have in your life. Being consciously grateful for the ability to think and feel is such a powerful exchange of energy with the Source of all life. And it is so simple! Ironically, the most seemingly complex concepts and structures in both the natural and synthetic worlds are built upon a foundation of intricately interconnected and interdependent simplicities. I feel that much of my own journey of life has been about unwinding all the complexity and confusion and discovering and appreciating the simple things. The road to this awareness has in many cases been filled with obstacles, challenges and traumas; yet, has simultaneously presented an abundant source of inspiration, creativity, self-healing and awakening.

You may be familiar with these aphorisms: 'As above, so below'; 'as within, so without'; 'as ye sew, so shall ye reap'. In truth, the way our external world manifests is a direct reflection of our internal state of being. Maintaining right relationship with the outer world is about discovering, understanding and accepting the gifts in those parts of our inner world that many spiritual people refer to as the 'shadow'. As I affirmed earlier, to truly know the way of peace is to meet all the aspects of the Self that are restless. Embracing the shadow self is a deeper process than simply naming those aspects of the Self which we find confronting. It is understanding that these parts of our character are tools for coming into true alignment with our being. When we fully engage with the shadow Self and experience the emotions that are triggered by our interactions with, and observations of, the behaviours of others, we are reminded that these instances are invitations, opportunities to expand our consciousness. By allowing the aspects of the Self to transform, you invite the love from the Divine to enter your heart.

Activity 3: Balancing Your Sacred Feminine and Masculine Energies

We all have an ability to become aware of the nature of the feminine-masculine energy interplay within our own personal space, and you need not travel all the way to Uluru to balance it! There is, however, one essential ingredient that will expedite the process of aligning your feminine and masculine polarities: direct physical contact with the Earth. Connecting directly with the natural surfaces of the planet neutralises the excess current that flows through our body from external stimuli; it facilitates the releasing of Electro Magnetic Radiation (EMR) and similarly inhibits our susceptibility to taking on EMR from our environment. In today's world, with the increase in wireless networks, Bluetooth devices and other hands-free and remote technologies, electromagnetic interference is particularly prevalent. This next activity allows us to reconnect with nature and the Earth in a simple, sacred and therapeutic way.

Step 1: Visit Nature

Find a beautiful place in nature that you are particularly drawn to or fond of - it may be a beach, rainforest, garden, cave, waterfall, lake, or any other natural structure that calls you.

Step 2: Work with the Stone Kingdom

In the nature setting that you are drawn to, you will look for two very distinct stones with which you are going to spend some time. The first stone you are seeking carries a feminine energy; its appearance is smooth, nurturing and healing, and its feel is delicate and soft. The second stone will be less smooth, possibly rougher in texture, and will emanate majesty and wisdom; it will emit an energy of protection. This stone will resonate with the masculine frequency.

The colour of the two stones does not hold any special relevance for the purposes of this activity; however, in my experience, the colour of the feminine stone has a gentler pastel hue, while the masculine carries a more rustic quality. Stones contain all the same types of minerals that are found in the human body, which is what makes journeying with them even more appealing. If you are already accustomed to working with stones, I trust that this activity will enhance your practical awareness of the healing power of the mineral kingdom; likewise, if you have not yet had the opportunity to spend any time with stones, this is sure to be a positive step towards aligning more with nature and the Earth.

Step 3: Balance your Feminine and Masculine Energies with the Help of Your Calibration Stones

You are in your nature setting, have searched for, and discovered, two calibration stones, one that has feminine energy, the other with qualities that resonate with the masculine frequency. This activity requires you to now select a starting point (which will also be your finishing point), from which you are going to move in either a linear or circular direction. For example, if you are at a beach setting, you may choose to walk along the beach; if you are in a rainforest environment, it may be that you can walk a circuit; for a garden setting, it may be possible to simply move around the garden in a circular direction.

Begin by holding your masculine calibration stone in your right hand, and the feminine stone in your left and commence walking in either a straight line or clockwise direction, depending on your setting. Continue walking in this direction for a duration of 11 minutes. While you are moving, intermittently swap the stones between your hands. Become aware of how the stones feel in each hand, particularly what feels comfortable and what is not so comfortable. Continue sharing the stones between your hands.

After eleven minutes, change the direction in which you are walking; this could be either walking anticlockwise, or backtracking to return to the starting point - this leg of the activity must also be at least 11 minutes in duration. Once again, continue to pass the stones between your hands. The goal with this activity, when repeated a number of times, is to get to a point at which you can no longer decipher which stone is in which hand, as they both feel somewhat the same. At this point you will have balanced the masculine and feminine aspects of your energy.

Comments / Notes / Observations

SEAN C. SULLIVAN

CHAPTER 6

Meditation: The Key to Understanding Energy

Retrospectively, I consider myself very fortunate to have been raised in an open-minded family, in which I was encouraged and nurtured as an individual. My father, in contrast, experienced a childhood that was very much aligned with the doctrines of Roman Catholicism; however, life experiences evolved his knowledge and awareness to a more universal and cosmically connected perspective on spirituality. It was this foundation of acceptance and diversity of belief systems that enabled me to explore my own interests in metaphysics and personal development later in life. I had become familiar with the word 'meditation' from a young age, my father having introduced me to a myriad of popular spiritual authors. In fact, even as a child there was something that resonated in me with Buddhist philosophy and, in fact, with most eastern spiritual practices. It was not until after the birth of my first child that the universe started presenting opportunities for me to fully experience the nature of meditation.

Ten months after our daughter's birth in 2010, Rachael and I had the pleasure of meeting, and undertaking a weekend course with, a beautiful clairvoyant lady, who happened to be a friend of a member of Rachael's extended family. Our connection and friendship with this wonderful lady continues to be a source of inspiration and wisdom for us both. Our friend had developed her own meditation methodology based on years of dialogue with the realm of spirit guides, ascended masters and archangels. Rachael and I learned a very simple way of experiencing visualisation, a particular form of meditation (there are many and varied types of meditation methodologies as we will discuss a bit later).

Subsequent discussions about my childhood, and various 'phenomena' that I had witnessed throughout my life, prompted the suggestion that maybe I would benefit from some formal training in energetic healing. This had certainly been an interest of mine, but I was unsure about the specific discipline that I wanted to study. I investigated Reiki, as this was probably one of the more familiar energetic healing modalities; however, I met a lot of resistance in my pursuit of both information and a mentor. At that point I affirmed that things would simply happen when they were meant to. Curiously, within three months, my affirmation to the universe was answered with incredible synchronicity.

At the end of every year, for as long as we have been together, Rachael and I have enjoyed spending some vacation time in Byron Bay, New South Wales. In January 2011, before our daughter's first birthday, we were browsing in some shops during our annual holiday in Byron when Rachael was approached by a local Reiki healer. After an intriguing conversation, the healer suggested that we might be interested to visit a certain crystal shop, not far from where we were, as he believed the crystals there held a high vibration.

With some time up our sleeves, Rachael and I decided to go in search of the shop and were pleasantly surprised when we found it. Just as had been described, the crystals did have a 'charged' vibration. While Rachael was engaged in conversation with the shop attendant, an older lady appeared from a back room and was immediately drawn to our daughter. She asked about our daughter's birthday and proceeded to offer a brief numerological and astrological reading. The lady subsequently proceeded to do the same for Rachael and me; the readings were, incidentally, extremely accurate. Rachael was intrigued about this interesting lady and happened to query the shop attendant as to the lady's name. When we heard her name, Rachael commented, "I know that name - there can only be one person with a name like that".

It turned out that Rachael's second cousin, the same one who had introduced us to the clairvoyant woman, happened to be a close friend of the lady we had just met. And, as synchronicity would have it, this lady was a shamanic healer and just happened to be offering a course in meditation and healer training. Well, something about these circumstances just resonated with me, and within a month, I was in my first meditation workshop as part of a 13-week energy healer training program. I was so excited. Was this the mentor and modality I had been waiting for? Feeling very intrigued, I approached my first class with both excitement and apprehension. When I arrived at the upstairs healing space, I felt very calm and peaceful. I somehow knew that this would be the beginning of an interesting and life-changing journey.

The Simpler, the Better

In my first ever meditation class, I was surprised to discover that the act of meditation was, in fact, somewhat easier than I had envisaged. To be honest, I believed that meditation involved having some profound experience; either I would have a visual epiphany or receive some unexpected audible message from a spirit guide. When neither of these anticipated outcomes eventuated, I was left wondering what the point was to meditation at all. I learned very quickly that meditation is concerned with minimising stress responses in the body. First and foremost, meditation is all about breathing. It requires us to simply bring our awareness to our breathing cycle, rather than trying to control the nature of our breathing. It was not until very recently that I fully understood exactly why conscious breathing is so important; I will share this with you a little later in this chapter.

My first meditation mentor would always say "we do not try to breathe; we are simply aware that we are breathing". Over a period of twelve months, I meditated for twenty minutes every morning. Eventually, I did start having visions and receiving intuitive guidance, but it took some time for that to develop. In the beginning, it was just a great feeling to be able to find a place of stillness and peace, amidst all the stressors that work, and family life, potentially presented. At this point, I would like to clarify that, although my meditation practice was twenty minutes in duration, you do not have to devote that amount of time to meditative practice. Similarly, there are numerous meditation practices that I have learned, and I would like to briefly discuss two specific processes that I have found quite useful in bringing me to a place of stillness and peace.

Visualisation: Bringing Images to Life

In my meditation and shamanic workshops, I have often tended to use the terms *visualisation* and *imagination* interchangeably. *Imagination* is the process of bringing an image to life in one's mind, not to be misconstrued with *pretending*, which is most accurately used in legal language to denote the deliberate falsification of information. Images that we visualise are often experienced as very real, as can happen in a dream state. In shamanic journeying, a particular type of meditative visualisation, it is quite a common occurrence to not only see things, but to hear sounds, smell aromas, taste flavours, and even feel the physical environment. One of the most effective self-guided visualisations I have experienced is a journey to my own garden, one that I create and can revisit at any time.

Activity 4: Creating Your Own Special Garden

Find a quiet place, where you can be seated comfortably without disturbance. Begin by closing your eyes and bringing your awareness to your breathing. With every breath you take, you bring just a little more calm and peace to your being. If you are feeling any tension or discomfort in your body, as you inhale allow your breath to travel to that area and exhale out the tension. Similarly, if you feel any restlessness or excessive emotional energy, simply allow your breathing to carry it out of you, so that you can be as peaceful as possible.

After a few minutes of deep, slow breathing, having allowed the stress and stagnant energy to leave your body and mind, visualise a pathway that forms in front of you. Walk along this pathway for a few breaths...you come to a descending staircase leading you down to a beautiful garden. This is a garden of your own creation, and it is your special place. Take note of any colours, sounds, smells, animals and any other magical things that you are experiencing. Spend a few minutes just observing and enjoying the surroundings.

When you are ready, simply walk back to the staircase you walked down, and return up the steps to the pathway. Walk back along the pathway until you come to your home, back to the place where you are seated, back in to your physical body. Be aware once again of your breathing and the sounds and smells of the environment. You may like to wriggle your fingers and toes to stimulate circulation and, when you are ready, slowly open your eyes.

Mantra Meditation

My first experience of mantra meditation was incredibly simple. A mantra is an affirmation – a word, sound or a phrase – that is repeated numerous times, enabling a hypnotic, meditative result. It is very useful, particularly with people for whom focusing on breathing is not enough to induce a deep meditative state. A mantra can be a simple 'Om', or it can be a complete phrase. The first time I experienced this type of meditation, I was guided towards a one-word mantra. More recently, I experimented (ironically) with the words 'a little more calm - a little more peace'. The experience was profound. I offered these words as a mantra for my wife in her daily practice; she reported that this mantra was "really beneficial" and helped her drop into a relaxed and peaceful meditation. Whichever words you choose to repeat, the objective is to bring your attention back to the mantra, so that it is your mind's focus for a set period.

At the Heart of Meditation

I mentioned earlier that my knowledge and understanding of the most fundamental benefit of conscious breathing was only a relatively recent acquisition. Well, I had always been intrigued by what science now considers to be the master organ of the body. I used to take for granted that the brain was the super computer of the human anatomy. However, when I dug deeper into physiology and further into the growing field of quantum physics, I discovered that perhaps I had been overlooking the role of potentially the most important organ in our bodies: the heart. For just a moment, I would like to emphasise some of the most crucial facts about the human heart, many of which I did not consider as significant until recent times. The human heart:

∞ Is responsible for circulation of oxygen and other nutrients to every region of the body;
∞ Is the first vital organ to develop *in utero*, even before the brain;
∞ Has its own electrical current, which it sources separately and independently of neural circuitry;
∞ Can survive independently for lengthy periods outside the human body;
∞ Resides at the centre of the body, two thirds on the left side and one third on the right side of the body;
∞ Energetically, sits in the middle of the seven-chakra system;
∞ Research has suggested that it omits a *Toric* field around itself that resonates at the same frequency of cyclical vibration as that detected around the Earth.

I would encourage anyone, whether from a spiritual or scientific viewpoint, to examine some of the latest quantum scientific discoveries, namely those concerning the human heart and its deeper physiological role in biorhythmic maintenance. In a peaceful, heart-centred space, we can find a sense of safety, allowing us to switch off our basic survival instinct.

These days, I get the impression that the clear majority of people with whom I come into contact is experiencing a relatively elevated state of fight-flight. However, it is mainly perceived, rather than actual threats to our survival, that tend to trigger our over-secretion of adrenaline. Our adrenal glands are working overtime, due not to our survival needs (which is the real function of our fight-flight mechanism); people tend to silently process their decisions and reactions, ever analysing whether they were right or wrong, continually critiquing themselves, deliberating over the past or hypothesising about the future.

Meditation in any form brings our conscious awareness to the present moment and reinforces the notion of quieting the mind chatter. Meditation is especially helpful for people with insomnia or those whose level of anxiety inhibits them having a night of restful sleep. In the course of my work as a shamanic healer and massage therapist, I was surprised to discover that there are actually some people that are in flight-flight even while they are sleeping. The result is that, unfortunately, these people awaken feeling tired. In meditation, we have the capacity to access the same brain waves that are normally programmed to engage while we are in a state of deep sleep. Taking this into consideration, a daily practice of meditation may begin to retrain the brain and mind, so that new sleep patterns can be formed.

It was comforting to recently discover that there are a number of early childhood and primary level educational institutions that have started to include meditation as part of their daily teaching routine. I am a strong advocate of the inclusion of meditation as a daily educational practice, particularly in secondary school settings. Having taught across both primary and secondary school age groups in the fields of Creative Arts and Languages Other Than English, I can comment, with a high level of certainty, that some form of meditation can mean the difference between ten minutes of relaxed breathing and visualisation and thirty minutes of solid work, and a 40-minute challenge just to get through 10 minutes of work, especially on a Friday afternoon!

Scientifically speaking, meditation has been shown to enhance the activation of neural pathways, enabling greater concentration and a deeper and more connected level of cognition. Coupled with other relaxation tools, like essential oils and music, meditation can become not only an outlet for deep relaxation, but also a foundation for deep healing, self-expression and creativity.

Aromatherapy and Its Benefits in Meditation

Fortunately, during my massage therapy studies, I had the opportunity to learn about clinical aromatherapy. I felt it important to include some information about the ways in which the positive effects of meditation can be further enhanced using specific essential oils and certain oil blends. The use of plants for medicinal purposes dates historically as far back as written records tend to go. Our indigenous ancestors were thoroughly connected to the natural world, a relationship from which, for the most part in the western world, we appear collectively to have almost disconnected. Of course, the methods by which plant nutrients are extracted have changed dramatically; in fact, the distillation of plants to produce concentrated essential oils appears to be only a relatively recent practice. Our ancestors lived in harmony with nature; understandably they had developed a deep knowledge of not only which plants could be used in the treatment of certain ailments (and where to find them in their natural habitat), but also how the plants were to be used in the most biocompatible ways to promote optimal health.

Nowadays, essential oils of all different types are readily available in pharmacies, health food stores, wellness centres, and online through multi-level marketing companies; what appears to not be as available is the correct theoretical information and practical educational processes that underpin their use in a safe and effective manner. In massage, essential oils are applied topically to the skin after dilution in a suitable carrier oil like coconut, almond or my personal favourite, jojoba. Carefully selected oils are used for specific reasons, for their effectiveness in facilitating improvement in physical and emotional imbalances.

One of the more widely and most recommended ways of using essential oils, is through diffusion into the air. When we inhale an aroma, this influences the olfactory nerve, which carries messages to the limbic brain. The limbic brain is the neurological area closely associated with memory, and the processing of emotion. In the healing of trauma and wounding, when coupled with meditation exercises, the therapeutic properties of certain essential oils can have a calming impact on the nervous system and have been shown to assist significantly with the release of stagnant physiological and emotional energy. Music has a similar role to play in shifting energy; in fact, it is so powerful that I have dedicated the entire next chapter to exploring the amazing healing power of sound.

Comments / Notes / Observations

_____

_____

_____

_____

_____

_____

_____

_____

_____

_____

_____

_____

_____

_____

CHAPTER 7

Sonic Resonance: The Fundamental Link between Music and Wellbeing

M usic has been, and continues to be, one of my most influential and valued life companions. To this day, my parents still remind me that, as a young child, I would be singing constantly (apparently even before I could talk). At the age of three, the elderly next-door neighbours used to make requests to my mother and father for me to visit of an afternoon and put on private vocal performances. My parents still reiterate how healing an experience those mini concerts were for our dear Scottish next-door neighbour, whose husband had passed away some years earlier. I do not personally remember those childhood recitals; suffice to say that my parents' early observations of how music could impact people no doubt had a lasting effect. After all, sound is now one of my own most readily used mediums for shifting energy related to emotional and energetic trauma.

The power of sound and music as a healing tool has been widely and intricately researched. Some of the discoveries are quite amazing. Before going too far into the nature of sound as a healing medium, I would like to point out that in the context of healing, I use the term 'sound' far more frequently than 'music', and this is a deliberate choice. During my university studies as an undergraduate Arts student, majoring in music and foreign language, I had adopted the familiar hypothesis that music was a 'universal language'. After all, it can be read and written like any other language and requires a reciprocal process of both giving (performance) and receiving (audiation) in order for the expression of music to be fully realised. After several years of working as a music educator, as well as other experiences I have had, I can offer with confidence that music is no more a universal language than English!

When I visited Ireland for the first time to connect with my father's family, and my extended family heritage, I happened to observe a conversation between two of my father's cousins. When asked for my opinion about what was being said, I innocently replied, "I'm sorry, but I don't speak Gaelic". Rather perplexed with my response, one of the cousins commented, "We weren't speaking Gaelic, Sean". As great a command that I believed I had of my native tongue, that did not help me at all in Ireland! Musical perception works in a fairly similar way. I can play a specific piece of music to a middle-aged northern Spanish person and evoke in them a feeling of patriotism, oppression, anger and sadness, while the same piece of music, when heard by a young person of Asian descent, yields limited, if any, emotional response. Music, unequivocally, evokes feelings and emotions; however, the nature of these responses is highly contextual. It is evident then, that the influence music has and the role it plays in our individual lives, is based on cultural, social and historical conditioning, and memories of personal life experiences.

Music and the Limbic Brain

One afternoon earlier this year, I came home from work in a relatively positive mood and discovered that Rachael had not experienced the same kind of day. She felt emotionally flat and I really wanted to try to lift her energy levels. I sensed the need for both of us to connect musically, and somehow, I managed to convince her to come with me to the keyboard to sing a few tunes. We spent perhaps a half-hour or so making music together, Rachael singing and me accompanying on the keyboard; the kids danced and sang with us. After we settled the children and tucked them into bed, Rachael was hanging the washing out on the upstairs line, and I noticed that her mood had changed dramatically (in a good way). "Wow!", I commented, "You seem heaps better". She replied, "Yeah, it's amazing how music can lift you up". This was an incredibly powerful observation, and one that is worth examining in more depth.

Just as the inhalation of diffused essential oils can affect the emotional centres of the limbic brain, so too can musical stimulus. In this instance, a 30-minute session of musical creation was enough to lift Rachael (and me to a certain extent) out of a state of stagnation. The limbic system is the part of the brain responsible for the processing and integration of emotions and has a significant role to play in memory functions, as well as numerous other cognitive processes. Incidentally, understanding the roles and responsibilities of the limbic brain is a significant component of the West direction of the medicine wheel shamanic training.

Music has the capacity to evoke nostalgic sentiments, and similarly has the potential to bring us to tears. Can you imagine some of those "tear-jerking" films without the underlying musical input? In fact, if I am totally honest, I would propose that music is the fabric that most deeply connects our emotions to what we see on a film screen. For argument's sake, let's offer here a simplistic definition of the word *music* as 'a collection of purposefully and methodically organised sounds'. Certain combinations of sounds presented at different pitches, tempos and intensities, appear to affect human beings in different ways. Music as a practical and theoretical discipline interacts with the brain and intellect; on a deeper level, it similarly communicates directly with the heart. We are now entering exciting discussion territory, and I would like to divert our focus away from 'music' back to 'sound'.

Sound is one of the most concentrated forms of vibration. I remember watching a television show one time that was dedicated to investigating the myth that concentrated sound, when performed at a certain pitch (measured in hertz), and a specific level of intensity (number of decibels), could shatter glass. I was convinced that it was merely a rumour, an old wives tale intended to have an impressive impact on the big screen. To my amazement, under strict test conditions, the glass did shatter, and the research team proved once and for all that, in fact, vibration with resonant properties, can indeed dramatically affect a solid structure. Similarly, I have observed the effects that the sound of the didgeridoo can have on water. I have played the didgeridoo adjacent to a bowl full of water; the water began to ripple. What can be deduced from these examples, is that concentrated forms of sound can affect change in the stability of both liquid and solid matter.

Based on my own experiences, I would go one step further and hypothesise that sound, when channelled in a very specific way, can be used to change, or redirect, the flow of energy. I recently provided a didgeridoo sound healing experience to a young lady from Sydney, who described the experience as a "massage for the internal organs". She felt the vibrational effects of the sound throughout her entire body. Why exactly is it, then, that certain sounds and sound combinations can have such an effect on us physically, emotionally and energetically? One theory, and quite a plausible one at that, begins its case with focusing on the human heart.

The Heart Song

One weekend during the North direction of my Medicine Wheel training, I travelled to Sydney, as Rachael and I have both often done during our shamanic education, to spend some time with our Inca shamanic mentor. I had immersed myself for two days, between theoretical learning, self-guided introspective processes, *pacha* work (we will discuss *pachas* in more detail in Chapter Nine) and fire ceremonies, and at the end of the second day of activities, at around 2:30am, I returned to my motel room for some much-needed rest. Although I felt tired due to a rather physically, emotionally and energetically intensive day, simultaneously, I could feel an adrenaline rush surging through me as I started my final reflective journal activity for the day.

I closed my eyes at 3am, intent on falling asleep; yet, I was restless. Whether I was revisiting the day's events, or anticipating what would follow, suffice to say that I was wired! I decided to focus on my breathing, surmising that by doing so, I would perhaps induce a state of deep relaxation from which I could more easily fall asleep. After a brief while – two minutes, perhaps – I unintentionally tuned into my heart beat. It was very loud, and I felt that the sound of my heart was about to overtake my conscious awareness. As I focused more deeply, I noticed that I was following the circulatory rhythm of my heart as it moved progressively around the four chambers. Sinking deeper and deeper into a meditative state, I eventually fell asleep. When I awoke in the morning, I could not contain the excitement that I felt. I reached for my journal and began to write. I had been audience to one of the most profound pieces of music I had ever heard; I had fallen asleep to the song of my own heart.

The Power of Beat

As we have already uncovered, the human heart regulates its own pulse; it has a constant beat that can be physically felt and audibly heard. In fact, the very first element that I taught to young children learning music is *beat*, because they could understand the notion that the heart beat is what keeps us alive, similar to the role of the beat in a piece of music. In almost all traditional Indigenous cultures around the world, the drum played a pivotal role, particularly in ceremonies and shamanic journeying; its low tone and hypnotic pulse could induce a state of transcendental awareness. During my teaching days, drum circles were an incredibly popular activity. Not only do they present an opportunity for a community of people to come together and learn a bit about music in a fun and non-threatening way, but similarly, and more powerfully, drum circles are a means for people to channel their feelings and emotions in a shared creative and expressive manner.

A teaching colleague and I started holding drum circle workshops for primary and secondary school-aged students; the success of these workshops sparked interest in drumming from both parents and teaching colleagues alike. I was even approached by the Principal of the school where I coordinated Performing Arts and was asked to lead a professional learning session for the whole school staff. The experience was amazing, and my colleagues looked thoroughly reenergised and uplifted after the session. Drumming is a fantastic activity for releasing energy, and it is an affordable and accessible option for expressing oneself in a musical way without undertaking intensive theoretical and practical musical training. A djembe drum is a great asset; portable and simple to play, it can be easily transported to any drum circle.

Sound and the Chakras

Singing is a similarly effective musical outlet; however, I have found that self-esteem, confidence and self-perception issues often challenge untrained vocalists, and perhaps discourage people from having their singing voice heard in any other environment beyond the home shower. Whereas the drum has certain appeal to the lower chakras, specifically the base chakra, singing or toning as it has often been dubbed, has in its favour the element of pitch, and can have very healing effects on the entire chakra system.

I have spoken briefly about chakras, from the perspective of power centres that hold certain characteristics as part of the whole energetic system. More specifically, chakras are the points where the luminous body anchors to the physical body, and subsequently feeds information into the central nervous and endocrine systems. In my early training as an energy healer, I was taught that the chakras each spin at a certain speed, thereby vibrating at a specific frequency.

There are myriad opinions and perspectives regarding the intricacies of the chakras and how they work. One hypothesis proposes that the chakras resonate in tune with the seven frequencies of the diatonic scale, commencing with C (256 hertz) at the Base chakra, all the way up to B, at the Crown. In contrast, others subscribe to the notion that the human heart responds to an energetic vibration that resonates at 528 hertz. Some schools of thought have proposed that the electromagnetic field around the Earth itself vibrates at 256 hertz, further highlighting the potential connection between the biorhythms of the Earth and the natural cycles of the human body. Tibetan sound healing commonly uses singing bowls tuned at varying pitches, for use with different chakras, which supports the notion that different centres correspond to different tonal vibration.

We have already visited examples of the effects of vibration on solid matter; another very tangible instance is the scientific principle of *resonance*, observed within the harmonic overtone series. When the note 'C' is played on a grand piano, it triggers other, differently tuned strings, to vibrate as well. Such a concept lends itself to further investigation into the nature of the relationships between different sounds. It would certainly be an interesting study in relation to the chakras, and indeed human cells.

Regarding the nature of resonance and the chakras within a healing context, the above information is not entirely conclusive, and simply presents a plethora of opinions held by other practitioners and researchers. To be totally honest, I can only really offer my own personal experiences, measured by what I have encountered with the energy of the chakras of my own clients. I have personally felt the chakras spin at different velocities; my sentient perception, however, indicates that the energy of the chakras creates a figure-of-eight pattern.

While the chakras may indeed move in a clockwise direction, they project an energy which simulates the horizontal infinity symbol. In Figure 2, I have included a picture to illustrate more clearly the nature of the flow of energy from the chakras that I have sensed during my shamanic healing sessions.

Harmony and Peace

What is the difference between harmony and peace? In musical terms, *harmony* is a blend of two or more sounds that, when heard simultaneously, brings about a pleasing or uplifting response. In contrast, *dissonance* is a combination of two or more sounds that, when blended together, creates a clash in harmony, or a displeasing response. We can apply this concept directly to people we meet, places we visit, foods we taste, and events we attend...pretty much anything we experience in life. But what constitutes a pleasing or displeasing sound? Is there general agreement about the characteristics of harmonious sound, or is this a subjective experience unique to the individual?

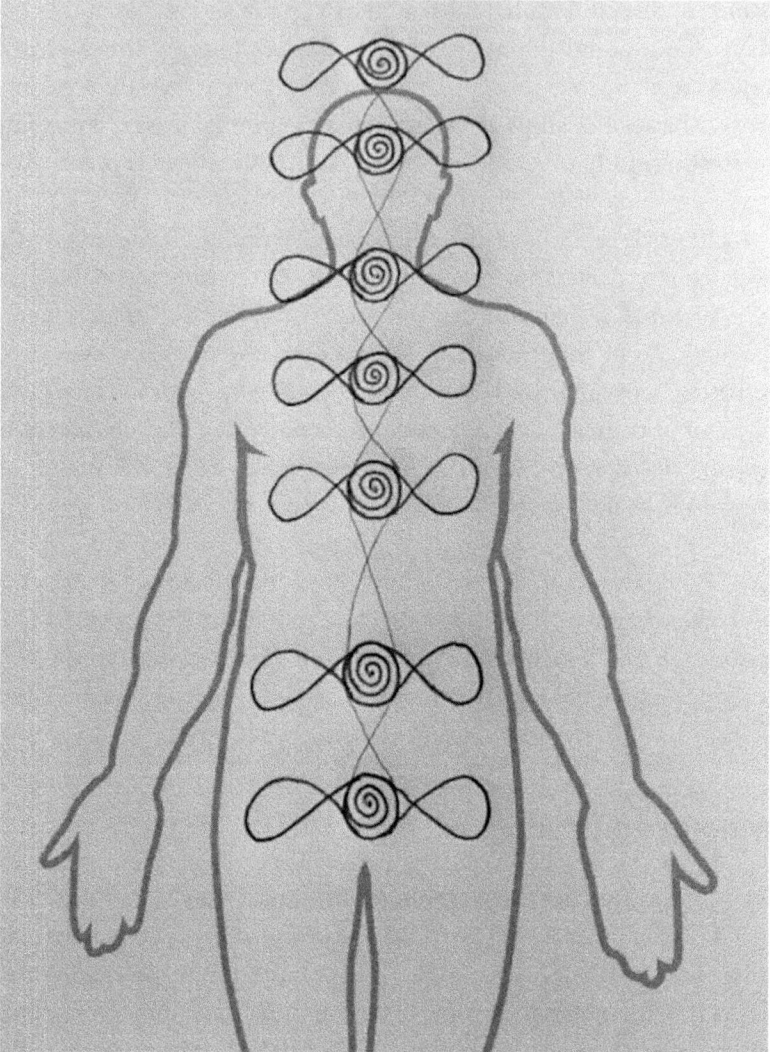

Figure 2: Flow of energy from the chakra centres

These are questions offered simply to promote further enquiry, and to stimulate potential future discussions. What I will reiterate with certainty is that, when we as individuals are living in harmony with all aspects of our own experience - with both our internal and external worlds - we create the perpetual, universal vibration of peace. Harmony is the resonance; peace is the result.

A Musical Gift for You

In 2011, I embarked on a creative musical project. I had been searching high and low for some healing music to include during my therapeutic massage sessions and shamanic healing programs. I had listened to samples of the many wonderful, relaxing musical creations of other composers of meditation and relaxation music on the market but could never quite find an album with which I fully resonated. With that in mind and fuelled by a desire to find appropriate healing sounds for my clients, I set an intention to receive some creative inspiration from Spirit, so that I could possibly compose meditation music of my own.

Some time went by after expressing my intentions to the universe, when one day, quite unexpectedly, I was tinkering on the keyboard, and I received an overwhelming influx of musical information. After about 15 minutes of continuous playing on the synthesiser, I had composed the scaffold for the first track of a three-part compilation, the Return to Earth guided meditation series. Shortly after, two other musical themes followed, and I now had the musical substance for a 3-CD series of guided meditation music.

Given my strong belief about the power of music and sound to create transformational shifts in energy, I believe it important to provide some samples of what I consider to be worthwhile healing sounds, as an adjunct to my written information. If you have physically purchased this book directly from me at a wellness event, or have attended one of the workshops, you will have been gifted a bonus CD. If you have purchased this book through one of the online bookstores, please visit the Trinity Wellbeing Solutions website for directions about how to access the downloadable sound files.

Irrespective of your musical ability or sociocultural background, sound is an irrefutably fundamental part of your life. I would encourage everyone to actively listen to music every day, be aware of the sounds you hear and your responses to them; and in some way, create meaningful sound for yourself daily, through playing an instrument, drumming, singing, humming, whistling or whichever way you find comfortable and practical. Imbed it in your healing regime in whatever fashion aligns with your lifestyle.

Comments / Notes / Observations

_____

_____

_____

_____

_____

_____

_____

_____

_____

_____

_____

_____

SEAN C. SULLIVAN

CHAPTER 8

Creativity and Self-Expression: Discovering the Inner Divine

My father and I often discuss the mystery scientists have encountered in their attempt to understand the unique structure of even the simplest things in life, like snowflakes. As my father comments, scientific investigation has yet to discover two snowflakes that are identical. Well, I had little knowledge about that area of research, and although it was quite a conceivable concept, I was admittedly a little uncertain as to whether Dad was on the right track. However, after further academic investigation, my findings appeared to concur with those of my father. It was similarly at that point that I reflected on my own historical observations.

As a secondary school student, and later as an educator, I was fortunate to have known quite a few sets of identical twins, both male and female. Despite ostensible similarities in physical appearance, it was always relatively easy to work out which twin was which. There was inevitably some small physical characteristic, personality trait, or a behavioural idiosyncrasy that would provide visible clues as to their identity. Although two things (people, leaves, stones, etc.) may appear superficially identical, every individual thing in existence is, in fact, a unique expression of creation.

I would go one step further now and propose that, following the hypothesis that all things are a unique expression of creation, if human beings are individually unique, then their expression of the energy of creation will also be unique. On that basis, I would argue that humans are innately creative beings, and we are all unique in the way in which the energy of creation manifests within us. More crucially, I am convinced that, to fulfil our life purpose, and fully realise our individual life path, we must unlock and unleash the creative energy and potential that reside in our DNA and luminous blueprint, and share that creative expression, in some way, with our external world.

I was discussing my ideas for this chapter with a dear and beloved friend of mine, and we just happened to start talking about the nature of creativity and its importance in the full realisation of a person. My friend was adamant that she was not creative. She commented, "I think I missed out on the creative gene". She had always considered herself to be mediocre in a creative capacity, never quite perfecting certain artistic endeavours, and in her eyes never able to find solutions to problems or come up with new innovative ideas, even in her studied fields. I reminded her that being inventive and expressing one's creative potential, are not the same thing. Inventiveness, by very definition, involves composing, building or making something from scratch, that has not been done before. Being creative, on the other hand, is simply having an avenue through which to express oneself artistically. I reminded my friend about how creatively she goes about socialising and networking with others, in both occupational and social contexts, not to mention the way in which her beautiful vocal skills have the capacity to captivate large audiences (you may have guessed that my 'friend' is actually my wife – Rachael is such a gifted vocalist!)

I believe it is our birth right, and in fact our destiny, to become co-creators of our world. Despite having explored spirituality through numerous different lenses, only after completing the East direction of the medicine wheel, could I fully understand the role creative processes have in the expression of one's soul. In a nutshell, we cannot be totally liberated until we have explored and expressed our creative potentiality.

From a personal perspective, I consider myself to be extremely fortunate to have come into the world with certain artistic tendencies. I have mentioned previously that music has always been present with me, and I have indeed found much fulfilment from both performance and compositional endeavours. That said, the intrinsic urge to engage in creative projects tends to pursue me in almost every aspect of my life. As I have reflected, the way in which creative and expressive inspiration unfolds is unique to everyone; however, in case you have not yet found your own expressive niche, or like me you love experimenting with new ideas, I thought I would share with you some of my own experiences, which you may (or may not) find helpful in discovering that part of you that is yearning to be fully realised. Please also remember, that *creativity* is not necessarily synonymous with *perfection*, so as you read about my personal creative projects, I encourage you to bear in mind that much practice went in to these processes before I considered myself either confident with, or competent at, any of them!

Jewellery-Making

A few years ago, when I had first contemplated participating in a wellness event, I had the idea in my head that I needed to have something other than 'healing' to offer people at my stand. Crystals and essential oils were an obvious inclusion; however, for some reason I felt that I needed to have some form of body jewellery available. I searched various avenues for some necklaces or pendants that I could include in my festival display. There are some rather beautiful sacred geometrical and crystal-based pieces out there; to be completely honest, I was just not resonating with anything that I had seen.

At that point, I really needed some guidance, so I entered a meditation one morning, with the intention to retrieve some amazing suggestion that would lead me in the right direction. Well, I was told that the reason that I had found it such a challenge to find a piece jewellery that resonated, is because I had not made it myself. That is all good and well, but I had not made jewellery before, and the concept felt very foreign to me. I asked for clearer guidance as to how I could possibly start making earrings and necklaces. When I concluded the exercise, and opened my eyes, the first thing I saw in my living room was the Native North American medicine wheel. I knew at that point that I was meant to use the symbol as creative stimulus for a pendant. Ironically, and quite synchronistic, I had already gathered many of the tools and materials that were needed to start the project. As the process of making pendants unfolded, so too did my intuitive knowledge of how to create other jewellery pieces. Soon I was making earrings, necklaces and dream-catchers.

Wood Craft

During my visit to Uluru, I had the honour of undertaking a very sacred journeying experience, during which I connected with some of the local ancestors, the wisdom keepers from the past, who remain guardians and protectors of the sacred sites around the Rock. During a silent ceremony with the ancient ones, I was given a precious gift - an intuitive message indicating that I needed to work with wood energy. I had seen a beautifully hand-carved wisdom stick in one of the art galleries near Uluru, and I became fixated on the idea of making something similar. Over the next six months, I worked for an hour almost every day, until finally I completed a carved serpent 'talking stick', which I now carry with me to workshops and ceremonies.

Culinary Art

Whether it is inherent Taurean nature, or an acquired interest in combining various food sources to create a taste sensation, it is evident to me that making tasty meals is undoubtedly one of my most rewarding and pleasurable creative endeavours. Not only can one engage colour therapy and aromatherapy simultaneously, but food preparation can be achieved in such a way as to promote cellular health and overall physical, emotional, mental and spiritual wellbeing. Curiously, food that has been made with passion and loving intent, tastes markedly different to food that has been made in a uniform way, simply because it is what happens to be on the menu.

Cleaning and Personal Care Products

This is by far the most fun and truly fulfilling experiment that I have dabbled with to date. And, of course, there is a story that preludes my experimentation with my own cleaning and personal hygiene products. People who know me well would no doubt be aware that I have very thick, fast-growing, Irish hair that, when it starts to become too long, grows up instead of back and down. For many years, I used any number of supermarket or hairdresser-sourced gels, waxes and putties, in an attempt to manage my hair's behavioural tendencies. I found that most, if not all, commercial products, contained some type of mineral oil, or other undesirable ingredient that I was intently hoping to avoid.

I started researching less synthetic alternatives and happened to come across a natural recipe for hair wax, which uses beeswax and shea butter as a base. The finished product works equally as well as commercially available options, with a long shelf life, and is affordable to produce. Not only is it enjoyable and inexpensive to make your own personal care products, like deodorant and body wash, but you are doing yourself and the environment a huge favour. Care does need to be taken, however, even when using certain natural ingredients. Formulating personal care products is a science as well as an artform. I am an advocate of organic cosmetic training programs, as these provide the necessary insight and information required to make safe skincare products that contain accurately measured quantities of ingredients that are pH-specific and within dermal limits.

Creative Writing

I am perennially grateful that human beings have a way of logically encoding our thoughts and feelings in written form. Putting pen to paper, whether in the form of a daily journal, poem, song, recipe, children's story, or other reflective writing process, is a great way to stimulate and channel creative flow. I authored a number of academic essays during my university studies; however, it was not until later, during my shamanic apprenticeship, that I really came to embrace the beauty of written reflection. If somebody had asked me ten, or even five years ago, if I thought I could potentially be embarking on a written project like this one in the future, I would probably have been extremely sceptical. In retrospect, the chain of events that resulted in my decision to start writing a book, could not have been more synchronistic and divinely orchestrated.

Restlessness to Creativity: The Transformation

At this point, I would like to reiterate that, like many people in the world today, my life has been a kaleidoscope of adventures, obstacles and potentially traumatic learning moments. My approach to understanding and transforming the energy surrounding my more challenging experiences, has been somewhat 'trial and error' based. Until very recently, even after the completion of my shamanic apprenticeship, I still felt a restlessness within me, a yearning to discover and express what I was truly passionate about, a desire to fully know the driving force that was keeping me focused on my personal life goals.

What I will express with conviction is that my perception aligned most significantly when fully recognised and embraced one specific creative process - the designing of meaningful wellness education programs. I now understand this to be the expression of my life pathway. To come into a place of wholeness and gratitude, and to step forward into the rest of your life in a conscious, living state of calm and peace requires a transformation from accepting the cards you have been dealt, the story that has been written about you. Instead, inspire yourself to become the artist of your own co-creative masterpiece, and however that manifests for you, be proud of your efforts and achievements.

At this stage, I invite you to take some time to briefly recap and review the various stages we have covered so far, from our initial understanding and identifying restlessness, to this point of discovering a passion or creative idea to express:

1. Explore, name and understand the origin of feelings of restlessness with certain aspects of your life;

2. Allow your masculine and feminine (yin and yang) energies to align and your power centres to be balanced by connecting with the Earth and communicating with the energy of your divine matrix;

3. Take some time to be still and to become aware of your breathing, using your breath to access that place of peace and divinity within you;

4. Listen to and participate in some form of music-making to enhance cross-cerebral interaction, and reconnect your mind with the resonance of the heart;

5. Tap into your unique potentiality to express yourself artistically, thereby opening the doorway to becoming a co-creator of your own reality.

Activity 5: Naming the Parts of Yourself that are Creative

It can be highly therapeutic to remind ourselves of our creative potentiality. In your reflective journal, I would encourage you to take some time to yourself to either identify and acknowledge the ways in which you currently express yourself artistically or list some ways in which you could potentially explore and nurture your creative attributes. It is ideal to undertake this activity in a nature setting; alternatively, you could combine this process with the earlier meditation activity, and travel to your special garden where you can perhaps connect more peacefully with the guidance from your higher Self. As with the other reflective activities included throughout this book, I have provided some space on the next page for any notes you would like to make, in the event that this book becomes your personal record for the purpose of these activities.

Transformation is not always the easiest road; it requires patience, tenacity and, above all, trust in a force beyond what can often be tangibly perceived with the physical senses. In personal development circles there always tends to be a significant focus on the cultivation of skills that heighten extra-sensory perceptual fields. While this is indeed one of the goals of living as a conscious being, it is imperative to understand how to integrate our energetic awareness with the physical nature of our experience and, more specifically, how to maintain a healthy relationship with the physical vessel that enables our worldly interactions – our body. In Chapter Ten, we will aim to connect more deeply with the physical nature of our being. Before we do, let's firstly recall our earlier discussions regarding the nature of restlessness, and, more specifically, the energy of wounds and traumas.

Comments / Notes / Observations

_____

_____

_____

_____

_____

_____

_____

_____

_____

_____

_____

_____

SEAN C. SULLIVAN

CHAPTER 9

From Wound to Gift: Transforming the Energy of Trauma

Make me an instrument of thy peace.

Where there is hatred, let me sow love;

Where there is injury, pardon;

Where there is doubt, faith;

Where there is despair, hope;

Where there is darkness, light;

Where there is sadness, joy.

-Prayer of St. Francis

The greatest gift that I have received during my medicine wheel journey, is the gift of understanding the nature of energy. One of the characteristics of energy is that it is not static; it is constantly moving and transforming. Every single experience we have is stored in our atomic matrix. Frequently, our experiences carry an emotional charge which can be extremely confronting; however, it is simply an energy with which we have formed, and often perpetuate, a certain relationship. Allow me to elaborate.

At the age of 17, I was hit by a car. I sustained multiple injuries that required hospitalisation for nearly 6 weeks. After three or four months of intensive physiotherapy, I had learned to regain the use of both my legs. I have never been able to expose my right leg to sunlight. Psychological investigation revealed that I had most likely 'suffered' from some form of Post-Traumatic Stress Disorder which, to this day, remains a contentious issue in my mind. Such a trauma undoubtedly left wounding; not only physical scars, but mental, emotional and energetic obstacles to process and release. It was not until my early thirties that I discovered the tools and strategies that would allow me to shift much of the energy that was still held in my lymphatic system in relation to that one life-changing event. What I did realise at a young age was that the key to my healing was in my hands; I had the power to choose how I carried the energy of my experience on all levels.

Consciously, I decided to get on with the job of healing. I chose not to engage with the vibration of anger or bitterness, and instead focused on the wonderful learning that I had received. This was by no means an easy road; I was still haunted by my own fears for up to 15 years after the accident. Subconsciously, some 17 years after the accident, during a kinesiology session, I discovered that, on a cellular level, I was still holding on to an emotional charge in relation to the incident, which had embedded itself in my lymphatic system. Clearing that imprint was an incredibly liberating experience, and it represented the final releasing of that trauma. Even after so much time, there was still a cellular memory of an emotional response that I had subdued. At that point, I made a commitment to facilitating others to experience the same liberation from trauma; to teach the skills and processes that enable one to step out of their limiting belief systems and restrictive definitions of Self.

Wellness education is not just a passionate interest of mine; I feel as though it is my life path. I believe every person has both a right and a responsibility to live as a being of love and peace. My initiation into the shamanic practice has opened my eyes to the fact that attaining such a state of being is not only possible but is our destiny. Except for a few highly evolved spiritual avatars, most of us start on the spiritual quest as wounded healers, searching for answers and yearning to be free of self-limiting beliefs, self-defeating patterns of destructive behaviour, toxic emotions and memories which have childhood, generational and karmic origins.

The shamanic path enables the tracking, processing and transformation of stagnant energy, so that we can begin to manifest our desired reality, becoming co-creators of our experience, rather than perpetuating an illusory world that has been created and handed to us by others. When we ground with the Earth and notice the signs and symbols that speak to us in the natural world, we start to live in harmony with the energy of creation; we can see more clearly the interconnectedness of all things and that we are an inseparable part of a cosmic superintelligence.

Archetypes and their Pivotal Role in the Healing Process

It was not until my mid-thirties that I fully understood the meaning of the word 'archetype'. A few highly-respected authors have dedicated a significant amount of time to examining the nature of what I identify as 'common archetypes' and how they influence human relationships and interactions. It is important at this point to highlight a distinction between mythical energetic archetypes that are received during shamanic rites of initiation, and common archetypes that play out in our everyday roles and relationships with others. I would like to discuss both archetypal categories in a little more depth.

Mythical Archetypes

During the ceremonial process of transmitting shamanic rites, an initiate is gifted seven archetypes by the shaman. These are energetic seeds that have been passed down from shaman to shaman for hundreds, if not thousands, of years. Their purpose is to facilitate access to broader and more expanded insight into oneself and one's own life experiences. In the Inca tradition, the shamans work with four animal energies and three luminous wisdom keepers, who have symbolic historical significance to the Inca lineage. Each archetype is energetically transmitted into a corresponding chakra (or power centre) during a rite of initiation, where it continues to grow, and becomes a powerful energetic companion.

The study of totem animals is particularly fascinating, and illustrates, mythically, how we can draw on the wisdom of our animal brethren for guidance. Sometimes there are major life decisions that need to be made and we may not be able to see clearly the most advantageous way of moving forward. In these circumstances, we can engage with the perceptual state of the hummingbird or the eagle and ask for the vision and wisdom that these archetypes may have about the situation. I have observed many instances of transformation resulting from communication with energetic archetypes.

Common Situational Archetypes

During my own journey of the medicine wheel, it was interesting to observe the nature of archetypes that presented in my own life, particularly in my interactions with others. At first, I wanted to believe that my personality was relatively consistent and did not vary substantially throughout my daily routine. When I really stood back and examined myself from a neutral point, it was clear that I was not simply engaging with different roles in my interactions, but that my personality was potentially affected, depending on the role I was undertaking. This was incredibly curious. Consider my self-review of the archetype of the leader: assertive, confident, convincing, driven and tenacious in their approach; position this next to the healer: empathic, patient, calm, humble and selfless.

Interestingly, I was to discover that my experience of these situational archetypes was inevitably my own projection of expectation, of how I believed other people thought I should behave in a given scenario. My shamanic work was going to uncover an even deeper level of understanding of the way archetypes influence our interactions. Just as some archetypal energies can facilitate an expansion of our awareness, as can be experienced with totem animals, others can be self-limiting and inhibit our evolution, and that of others with whom we interrelate.

Archetypal Entanglement

Throughout my Medicine Wheel training, in my one-on-one sessions and group workshops, the nature of archetypal entanglement in relationships has presented as a significant contributing factor in the perpetuation of unwanted patterns of behaviour. The dynamic of one example of archetypal entanglement depicts three specific interdependent roles. These archetypes have no doubt been articulated and examined in the work of many other authors and spiritual teachers: *perpetrator*, *victim* and *rescuer*. In the cycle of entanglement, each individual archetype feeds off the energy of the other two. Although, at first, it may seem that the *rescuer* archetype is a potentially positive role, if you are engaging in any one of these archetypal roles, you are ultimately feeding the energy of all three. Allow me to clarify.

When Rachael and I got married, we agreed that we would equally share all the responsibilities of our life together. In 2009, we decided to expand our family, and the following year we welcomed the arrival of our first child. The demands of parenting became somewhat overwhelming, and within less than two years, we welcomed our second child into the world. With two young children at home, my lovely wife was inundated with homely chores, while I continued to work full-time. Now, it is not that either of us intended things to pan out this way, but I ended up taking on board all the financial decisions for the family unit. My beautiful partner usually appeared preoccupied, or even disinterested in the 'business' side of life. Accordingly, I simply continued to manage the incomings and outgoings.

During one of the activities of the East Direction of the Medicine Wheel, I felt intuitively that I had been playing the role of financial rescuer, and that my wife was, in fact, a victim. Both she and I had been contributing to the perpetuation of a certain dynamic in our relationship; my wife was simply taken care of, without any sense of awareness of the actual financial needs of the family unit. In fairness to both of us, we could not continue this arrangement.

I started to wonder how my wife would manage in the event that anything unexpected were to happen to me. The only way to empower both of us was to ensure that we were both involved equally in the household financial movements. We could then step outside the triangle, and no longer hold each other in a place of disempowerment. Bringing archetypes to our conscious awareness is a very powerful process. It can be challenging to acknowledge that an archetypal role is playing out, particularly when you are stuck in the dynamic.

Myriad Ways to Perceive the Same Trauma

Whatever stage you are at in the healing process, you never stop encountering experiences that deepen your understanding and wisdom of the journey from wound to gift. Just as you start to think that you have mastered the art of transcendence, another test is sent to strengthen your spirit. Does this sound familiar? In the middle stages of writing this book, I was presented with an experience that further advanced what I had thought to be an already considerable experiential awareness of the impact of motor vehicle-related trauma. Before I share that story, I would like to emphasise that an accidental trauma (i.e. one that does not fall into the model of the Victim-Perpetrator-Rescuer dynamic) can be experienced from any number of different perspectives. Consider my own personal example of a 'car accident', and the various points from which the trauma associated with such an incident, could manifest:

∞   The person who was physically injured;

∞   The one who was driving the vehicle that inflicted the injury;

∞   A passenger in the motor vehicle;

∞ The friend of the injured party who witnessed the impact;

∞ The first aid person, police officer or ambulance personnel who arrived at the scene to comfort and support the injured party;

∞ The parent or partner who received a disturbing phone call in the middle of the night, whose trip to the hospital was the longest and most apprehensive one they have ever made;

∞ The doctor who facilitated emergency triage treatment to the injured party and provided explanations to family members.

This is a small list, but you get the gist of where I am going; depending on the severity of the trauma, there may be several different layers of impact that a traumatic accident can have. The important observation is that each experience comes with a level of trauma that, unless resolved or transformed, can result in an unconscious emotional wounding or an imprint in the luminous energy field.

At 16 years of age, I witnessed a mini bus, travelling at 110 kilometres per hour, pull suddenly of the road and hit a tree, causing it to flip over a number of times before landing overturned on a bank beside the highway. The man driving the vehicle was one of my teachers, and the passengers were secondary school student friends of mine. We were returning home after a week-long tour of the east coast of Queensland. I was the first person to arrive on the scene, having almost leapt out of the car in which I was a passenger, in a desperate attempt to help my travelling companions. To cut a long story short, I pulled some of my friends to safety, tried to comfort those who sustained injuries and observed my teacher fall into a catatonic state of shock as the ambulance officers tended to him. The emotional impact of that experience was etched in my memory for quite some time after.

A year-and-half later, I was hit by a car, and subsequently understood the trauma associated with sustaining direct physical injury as a result of a motor vehicle collision. Almost nine years later, towards the end of 2003, I was riding my motorcycle to university in my final year of a Bachelor of Education program, when I was hit from behind by a four-wheel-drive, catapulting me over the bars and into the middle of one of the busiest roundabouts in the city. My motorbike was a write-off and I sustained lower back injuries that required physiotherapy for some time. Can you see an experiential pattern emerging here? Well, I am sure you have been anticipating the next part of my learning about the nature of motor vehicle trauma. I wrote this part of the book on literally the same day that the following events occurred. I was neither expecting, nor prepared for, what happened that day.

I drove out of my driveway and headed off to work for the family business, as I have done most days for the last seven years. By all measurements, it was a typical start to the day, as I took off up the street, admiring the glorious sunshine and stunning blue sky. I turned the corner into one of the backstreets and accelerated down the hill. Traveling now at around 50 kilometres per hour, I drove through a cross-intersection about 100 metres down from where I had turned into the street, when out of my peripheral vision I saw a push bike rider speed out of the side street to my left. I had enough time to move slightly to my right, but neither I, nor the cyclist, could take evasive action quickly enough, and the bike rider collided directly with the rear left-hand side of my car. I could hear and feel the impact, as the back wheel of the bike slid under my car's back wheel. The rider looked like a rag doll in my rear-view mirror and, as I pulled my car over to the far side of the road, I was unsure what I would encounter as I jumped out of the vehicle.

I could feel the adrenaline pumping through me as I ran, multiple anxious expletives exiting my mouth, towards the injured man who had ended up lying in the middle of the road. Luckily, he appeared to have escaped major injury, sustaining only cuts and abrasions. The reason that this accident occurred and how it could have been prevented are not the purpose of its inclusion in this piece of writing; as has been illustrated so far, I believe that life experiences are neither superficial, nor coincidental. What it does illustrate clearly is the role that *I* played in this powerful transaction, and how it builds on a history of similar events. Earlier in life, I had been both the observer of a traumatic accident, and the injured party.

This time, I was driving a vehicle that collided with another road user. This accident was as much about my own healing journey as it was a learning experience for the cyclist.

The Story I Tell Myself About Myself

Understanding the archetypal energy of the serpent is a fundamental component of the south direction of the Medicine Wheel. The serpent teaches us the lesson of shedding old skin, to allow for new layers to form. Letting go of the old, worn out version of ourselves, with its self-limiting beliefs and unproductive behavioural patterns, allows for the emergence of a new upgraded version of not only how we see ourselves, but similarly how we are perceived by others.

In 2015, I had the great pleasure of meeting one of my now good friends, colleague and soul sisters. During one of our many in depth philosophical and esoteric conversations, I heard the following phrase: "the story I tell myself about you is..." In their simplicity, these words opened a profound dialogue about the nature of the stories we all tell each other about each other, and about the world in which we live. Due to my personal journey, I became very interested in the way in which people both look at themselves, and similarly define their existence.

I began to observe all the people in my immediate circles and started a categorical list of the stories people tell themselves about themselves. The learning was amazing! Some people appear to define themselves by their occupation or career, deriving meaning in life from what they do in their paid employment. Others benchmark their self-worth by the quantity and / or quality of material possessions and wealth they have accumulated. There are those who are convinced that they are in fact a culmination of the multiple roles that they undertake throughout the course of a day: Mother, wife, sister, housekeeper, cook, cleaner, first aid officer...the list goes on and on. I have observed how some people's lives are so heavily influenced by the opinions of others. Evidently, some people even define themselves by their own suffering.

So, at this point, there are a few questions that I would like to propose to you, the reader, as they are questions that I have put to myself. Firstly, what is the story you tell yourself about yourself? And, secondly, is this the story you will continue to tell yourself for the rest of your life? And, finally, at the time of transitioning from this world to the next, is this the story you will still want to be telling yourself about yourself, or are there aspects of the script you would alter?

We have the ultimate power to co-create our world by remapping our way forward. We need not be limited by the past, nor by the expectations of others, or even by our self-imposed views derived from societal and familial influences. There are processes available to us that can facilitate change and transformation, provide great insight and wisdom, and can give us the courage to be guided by the heart, gut and head, rather than just the head alone.

Activity 2: Creating a *Pacha* – Working with Mother Earth

Pacha comes from the native Inca language, Quechua, and translates as 'place', or more accurately, 'space'. We work with pachas frequently in shamanic processes as they provide a sacred canvas to symbolically and creatively externalise, illustrate and manipulate the workings of our inner world. Similarly, a pacha enables us to welcome in the help of nature to release stagnant energy and allows us to reorient our perspective in relation to our life experiences.

A pacha can be created in a garden, park, forest, beach…anywhere you can connect with the Earth. In fact, some of my medicine wheel pacha work took place in public parks, vacant lots and even on downtown footpaths of some of Australia's capital cities (the medicine wheel is the self-driven journey the shaman takes in their shamanic apprenticeship, in which they transform from their beginning state of the wounded healer, to the place of the sage or self-referencing visionary).

In Chapter 4, we concluded by taking note of approximately 5 aspects or areas of your life, with which you may have experienced feelings of restlessness, or a dimension of your life with which you may need to shift your relationship. Essentially, the key to self-healing is concerned with repairing or upgrading the nature of our relationship with our life experiences.

Figure 3: A visual example of a pacha

Step 1: Opening Sacred Space

Before creating a personal pacha it is important to open a sacred space around you. Traditionally, shamans would open sacred space in their native language, giving thanks and gratitude to the four Cardinal directions, call in any archetypal or spirit energies from which they might be seeking guidance, and offer a prayer of gratitude to Mother Earth and Father Sky for providing a ceremonial space upon which to journey. The method one adopts to open sacred space is a personal choice. I have learned scripted prayers, both in English and Quechua, that I will often use before fire or water ceremonies; similarly, I may sometimes just open space by setting an honouring intent or blessing. Whichever way resonates with you is perfect.

Step 2: Create a Protective Circular Boundary

Now that you have opened the space, let's create a boundary of protection, a circular border on the Earth in which you can create a sand painting, a symbolic illustration, the process through which I will guide you as we continue. A couple of observations need to be made before we proceed:

1. The circular boundary, and in fact anything we place inside the pacha, must be combustible;

2. In addition, it is important not to remove anything from a living tree or plant; flowers, leaves, fruit and other items of nature must have fallen from their source of their own accord;

3. Lastly, working with Earth energies is a beautifully reverent process, and must be undertaken with gratitude and humility. Remember to connect with every twig, every leaf, every flower, every item, asking for its permission to be part of your pacha.

With these things in mind, you are ready to create a protective border, which will outline the canvass for your sand painting.

Step 3: Working with your Pacha to Release Stagnant Energy

After having set our intent for the use of our space, and building a protective boundary, we can really start to work with the energies of nature and call on the Earth elements to facilitate our healing journey. It is sometimes at this point when a little voice is heard in our heads that says, "how is the Earth possibly going to help me release my issues?" The first time I worked with a pacha, I was similarly rather sceptical about the process. I guarantee you that, as I surrendered to the moment, and allowed the elements of nature to play with the energy in the collage that I had created, I could start to see very clear teachings and gifts from the Earth. Every person for whom I have held space while undertaking pacha work, has gained some insight into their lives; in a few cases, the information has been life-changing.

On that note, it is time now to recall the list that you put together in Chapter 4, which categorically summarised the parts of you, or your life, with which you feel a sense of restlessness. Inside your circular boundary, physically mark (with sticks, leaves, etc.) each seven-year segment of your life (hint: the older you are, the more segments you will have). For example, if you are 39 years of age, you will have 6 segments in total. Now, bring your attention to the first aspect of restlessness on your list. In which seven-year phase of your life did you first experience this feeling or belief system? Choose a stick that represents that feeling or belief, and physically blow the energy of your restlessness into the stick. Whatever is internal within you that needs to be released, do it now by bringing it out from inside you and releasing it into the stick. You may feel it necessary to blow into the stick more than once to really get the energy out. When you are ready to continue, place the stick in the segment that corresponds to the age you were the first time you experienced this belief system or feeling. Now repeat the process for the remaining four feelings or beliefs.

Step 4: Upgrading Software

Releasing old patterns is easier said than done, right? Well, not necessarily. All too often people let go of old patterns of behaviour or habitually repeated activities, without upgrading their software. I shared a story earlier about App upgrades on the Apple Store. Now think of a computer software program that you might use regularly. Your program has functioned well, but over the last few months you have noticed that when it is used for too lengthy a period, it corrupts, and you need to shut the program down. Your device has often prompted you to download an update, and the corruption can be very frustrating.

There are three options available to you at this point:

1. You can continue using the corrupted program that keeps malfunctioning, and run the risk of compromising your whole operating system;

2. You can remove the software program and reinstall the same version of the program again; OR

3. You can remove the software and download the most recent version, which theoretically has had improvements made to it, to avoid similar issues from recurring.

When we release old patterns, it is imperative that we upgrade to a new behavioural program, thought process or 'habit' and set this intention emphatically, so as to inhibit the corrupted default software uploading again.

For each aspect of restlessness that you have identified, have blown into the sticks, and released into the pacha, select another stick that represents the upgraded energy that you want to insert in its place. For example, if you have identified dissatisfaction with your occupation or career, see yourself enjoying your work (this may well be in the form of a different workplace, or undertaking an alternative occupational endeavour). Choose the most energetically or emotionally charged, restless aspect of your life, and let's work with this one first. Really visualise and set the intent for what the upgraded version will be and blow the energy of that into the stick. Place the stick in the segment of your pacha which represents the current phase of your life.

Now repeat this process for each of the remaining aspects, ensuring ample time for visualising and setting the intent for transformations. You may wish to bring colour, sound or other mediums to inject life and energy into this part of your pacha. Once you feel happy with your pacha, allow it to incubate for the exact number of nights that there are segments in the pacha. If there are six segments in your sand painting, it is likely that it will need six day-night cycles to sit with the elements.

Step 5: Visit Your Pacha

Be sure to spend some time with your pacha daily, if possible morning and evening. Note any change or movement inside the circle; it is not uncommon for sticks to have either moved or been removed. It can help to keep a running journal detailing your observations and experiences, as well as any feelings or reflections that come up for you. Every individual person's first encounter with the pacha activity is unique.

In 2015, I was fortunate to host and co-facilitate a shamanic retreat at a beautiful bison farm, just south of my home in northern New South Wales. A colleague and I were joined by seven others, many of whom were healers, psychics or had been spiritually active for some time; however, the pacha was an unfamiliar process to all. It was a two-day retreat, and we were blessed with a mixture of elements, including a gentle shower of rain over night. Although the pachas had only been incubating for one night, the stories that were shared the following day brought both excitement and validity to the process.

The truth is, a pacha is the perfect canvas to illustrate just about any challenge we have in life. We can also create a pacha that is not about releasing stagnant energy, but rather about giving and setting positive intentions, particularly for planetary and universal healing. This can be a truly beautiful gift to the Earth. We do, however, always need to remember that we are dealing with energy and must remain in our integrity above all else. My shamanic mentor would often emphasise that we never set the intent to release energy on behalf of somebody else. In other words, your pacha is for your own healing, and should not be mixed with the energies of other people, even if you think that trying to create change in another person will benefit your situation. Manipulation of another's energy without their knowledge or permission is considered by many to be a form of sorcery and may have unfavourable ramifications. Holding the unconditional intent for the highest good for yourself and the universe is the perfect vibration to emanate during pacha work.

Step 6: Dismantle Your Pacha

Once your pacha has spent sufficient time receiving the energy of nature and playing with the elements, and you have drawn enough insight and information to find the gift in your experience (which is simply about shifting your relationship with the energy you hold regarding the restlessness), it is time to dismantle your pacha, starting with the items that made up the seven-year segments, and then moving out to the protective boundary. Ensure that you collect all items, leaving the space how you found it prior to commencing your sacred work. Once again, thank the Earth for holding such beautiful and connected space for you, and give gratitude to the energies you first called in for protection and guidance.

Step 7: Hold a Fire Ceremony

Fire is a powerful, transformative element. Traditionally, fire ceremonies could be held for any number of reasons, and presented a ritualistic platform, from which to honour and make offerings to the Earth mother, in addition to providing a medium for energetic transmutation. Ceremonial fires can be lengthy events, sometimes lasting several hours in duration. For our purposes – releasing the pacha and transforming the stagnant energies into a light vibration – we will keep this fire ceremony process very simple. You will need the following items before commencing:

- ∞ Access to a fire pit or brazier;
- ∞ Sticks and kindling;
- ∞ Firelighters / matches / BBQ tongs;
- ∞ The combustible items from your pacha.

Figure 4: A sacred ceremonial fire

Just as you did before you commenced work on your pacha, it is important to open sacred space by inviting the protection and guidance from guides, teachers, ascended masters, archangels and the Source of all that is. In the Inca shamanic tradition, an offering of Agua de Florida, or other sweet water, would be blown into each cardinal direction while the archetypal energies that symbolise each direction are called upon; this offering is extended to the Earth Mother and the Sky Father - the givers of life.

Once the fire has been lit, allow the flames to really grow, until you feel guided to add the contents of your pacha. As you do so, hold the intention for any stagnant or stubborn energy to be released into the light. After you have given your pacha to the fire, draw some light energy from the fire into the navel power centre, then the heart chakra, and finally the third eye and crown power centres. You may also like to blow some energy into a different stick and dedicate it to the healing of Mother Earth. Once you have concluded the ceremony, and the fire has burnt down, close sacred space by thanking the energies that you called in during the opening; this allows any celestial and archetypal visitors to return to their respective realm.

In traditional ceremonies, it was the fire-keeper's responsibility not only to maintain the fire during the ceremony, but also to remain with the fire until it had stopped burning. During my Medicine Wheel training, I recall a fire ceremony in which I participated in Melbourne, with a group of fellow shamanic apprentices. Our mentor had delegated key responsibilities to each of us – one of the group was given the role of fire-keeper. When the ceremony had concluded, I left the circle and joined my mentor for a late dinner. I found out the next day that my fire-keeper colleague had stayed with the fire until 6am. I felt relieved to have had the role of opening and closing sacred space!

Wellbeing and Connection with the Earth

The indigenous ancestors across the globe had an innate sense of connectedness to the Earth and lived in harmony and communion with the natural world. Our western way of life has progressively distanced itself from the natural environment. More and more we wear rubber-soled shoes, sleep on thick foam and metal-based mattresses on the second floor of our insulated, air-conditioned dwellings; we eat increasingly synthetic-based, microwaved foods and use potentially harmful, artificial chemically-enhanced personal care products. And yet, we scratch our heads in wonderment as to why there has been such an increase in disease and chronic illness in recent times.

As you continue to engage with processes like those described in this book, you will no doubt discover for yourself the crucial role that reconnecting with the Earth plays in our personal physical, mental and spiritual wellbeing. I trust you have enjoyed your experience of creating a pacha. This process becomes the foundation for understanding how to find a place of balance in our lives. We move now to further explore the nature and subtle language of the physical body.

Comments / Notes / Observations

Comments / Notes / Observations

SEAN C. SULLIVAN

CHAPTER 10

Built to Heal:
The Human Body's Repair Software

The human body is programmed with repair software. Consider when we accidentally graze our knee as a child. Firstly, the wound bleeds, in order to cleanse the area, and flush out any foreign debris. The capillaries usually constrict and a clot forms, eventually resulting in a hard scab that protects the wound. Then the skin cells busily prepare a new layer of skin under the scab, which eventually falls off when the new skin is ready to be exposed. Our cells know what to do! I would like to step back in time again, to 1995.

Six weeks after my disagreement with the motor vehicle, I was discharged from the Royal Brisbane Hospital and returned home. The future looked rather uncertain, and the road ahead undoubtedly appeared to be full of challenges. I was informed that part of my treatment as an outpatient would be attending a two-hour physiotherapy session twice weekly until deemed necessary, to facilitate my rehabilitation.

You see, I had not been able to walk since the accident; my legs had been in plaster back slabs, then a pressure garment, and post-surgery I was instructed to keep my right leg elevated whenever I was stationary to enable appropriate atrioventricular blood flow. The muscles in both my legs had atrophied significantly, and I had lost all muscular control below my right knee. It was a strange enough feeling to have no peripheral sensation; it was even more confronting to not be able to wiggle my toes. The physiotherapy programme was satisfactory, but to me was not enough for me to get back on my feet as quickly as I wanted. I remember a point in my recovery when I decided that the only way I could maintain any hope of regaining full function of my body was to start with the most peripheral point of my anatomy and will it to move.

Every day for about 10-15 minutes, I would focus on nothing else but flexing my right big toe. I continued this for some three or four weeks, until one day, quite surprisingly, (and rather painfully), my big toe responded. This was by far the simplest, yet most profound achievement in my healing journey. At that moment, I figured that if my tenacity to move one toe could result in the reactivation of supposedly damaged or dormant nervous circuitry, to the extent that my toe actually moved, I could potentially replicate that same process anywhere in my body. And so, began a totally revised vision of my body's innate capacity to mend.

Physical Pain and Discomfort: The Human Body's Caution Software

I recently attended a First Aid refresher course which, in Australia, is recommended to be undertaken once every three years. During the workshop, the instructor commented on the notion of pain, and his observations strongly resonated with my own. He commented that "pain is the body's warning mechanism. It indicates that something is physically not quite right". While pain is understandably a response that most people would prefer to avoid, some painful moments do result in incredible gifts. Now, I had thought about including some cliché in here about childbirth; however, I have no personal experience of birthing. In fact, in cases that I have witnessed, the trauma of the whole process, from pregnancy to labour and birthing, is immeasurable. Instead, I would like to share some further developments from my own personal healing journey.

After some time working in a somewhat sedentary occupation, my role changed, and I was given some additional responsibilities, which required a certain amount of manual handling. As time went on, my fitness improved, and the benefits of a more active work program had resulted in weight loss, increased energy levels and better sleeping patterns. After about two years, I developed a dull ache in my right hip and lower back. Self-diagnosis put this pain down to complacent manual handling techniques. My body was certainly communicating with me and I started to think more consciously about my body position when completing physically demanding tasks. Although I had revised my postural habits, my aches and pains had not improved and after 5 months of silent suffering, I finally decided to take a visit to a chiropractor.

Despite the relatively controversial attention that chiropractic professionals had historically received, I believed that, through some type of manual adjustment, my level of physical comfort could be improved. It turns out (which came as no surprise) that my postural issues most likely commenced as a result of the impact from the car accident. The physical work activities in which I had recently participated were enough to take my already compromised sacroiliac joint past its threshold. Clearly one too many traumas can push the body past its limits; unfortunately, at that point, the symptoms are more stubborn to treat.

After several chiropractic sessions, coupled with some targeted exercise, building core strength and flexibility, my body is now responding well to the way it has been treated (or neglected!) for a number of years. Now, what if I had been attuned to the language of my body far earlier in life, and was able to listen to the subtle way in which my body was communicating with me as a younger person? Perhaps I could have avoided this most recent discomfort!

It All Starts with the Cell!

It is intriguing the way the universe talks to you when you are receptive. I had been experiencing a high level of frustration with my saltwater swimming pool at home; it seemed to be in never-ending need of more chlorine, more algae-killer or more salt. I could never seem to keep up with its demands for some form of chemical intervention. After several months of experimentation with pH levels and cleaning processes, it suddenly dawned upon me that I had overlooked something very simple. I heard an internal voice state very clearly: "It all starts with the cell".

Funnily enough, I had been asking the universe for some obvious physical signs as confirmation of the phenomenal information about cells that I had been studying. One of the most resounding insights that I would like to share is the way in which human anatomy and physiology has traditionally been perceived within the Western medical paradigm, versus the body's actual potential to be fully capable of cellular recuperation, regeneration and even transformation achieved through very basic methods and without harsh external intervention.

Consider the following observed information about an individual, fully-functional cell (I use the word 'cell' generically here, as there are various types of cells of different shapes and sizes, which are created for very specific anatomical objectives):

∞ An individual cell understands its function as part of the greater whole, does not question its purpose and fulfils its role to the extent of its ability;

∞ A cell communicates openly with other cells with which it comes into contact, and exchanges (gives & receives) information with other cells unconditionally;

∞ A cell consumes only as much energy as it needs to undertake its activities;

∞ A cell works in a community to ensure the most optimal environment.

If our cells collectively go about their existence whole-heartedly in this manner, and we are but an intricate collection of these cells, why then do we as the collective find it so hard to act in the same way as our cells?

Science has demonstrated that at the heart of all matter is light. Logically then, at the centre of the smallest unit of matter as we understand it, there is light energy. What if humans could become so attuned to their physical and energetic makeup, that they could sense and even communicate with themselves at an atomic level? The questions I pose here are, for now, rhetorical in nature, and hopefully provide stimulus for further enquiry. I will say that there is a small number of medicine people that are pioneering this type of quantum healing in their work; and the effects are mind-blowing. Imagine a world in which all beings were totally balanced at the level of the energy within each atom...

Listening to the Language of the Body

The body talks directly with us every day, and the communications are often very emphatic. What appears to really be out of alignment, is our listening skills or, more specifically, our intuitions in relation to our body's both subtle, and sometimes plainly obvious, signs of stress. Over the past few years, as you will no doubt have already gathered, I have spent a phenomenal amount of time contemplating the nature of stress, particularly as it relates to the manifestation of illness and disease. Further to my previous discussions on the nature of stress, through factual clinical research findings, I discovered that only 1 per cent of physiological disease is causally attributed to genetic predisposition; in fact, 99 per cent of physical illness may very well be induced by environmental stress. At this point I would like to revisit the notion of energy and how it is held in the ethereal body.

Remember that, according to numerous modern and ancient spiritual traditions, human beings as physical structures are surrounded by an energetic matrix, which contains our blueprint, as it were, and this directly influences our physical experience. My shamanic ancestors affirmed that, despite our lineage and familial tendencies, we are not necessarily destined for a certain health complication simply because it is in our family history.

The reality is that, despite our genetic endowments, environmental circumstances and our own beliefs and choices as to the way in which we carry energy, will ultimately determine our individual level of wellness. So, how can we maximise our optimal state of well-being in our everyday lives? Let's start by exploring some of the proactive things we can do with our bodies to promote positive health; then I will conclude with an activity that may be useful in getting to know the subtle communicative mechanisms within your own body.

Are We Simply What We Eat?

This is not a trick question, and the answer is, of course, no! Wellbeing is a culmination of factors, one of which *does* happen to be what we put into our system. Over the last, perhaps, 15 years, I have observed several trendy fad diet solutions on the market, all offering the greatest weight-reduction and energy-enhancing promises. And no doubt these have had a significant level of success for some people. A couple of years ago, I subscribed to a health program that appeared fantastic at the time; unfortunately, it turned out to not be for me. People do not all share the same cultural heritage, environmental upbringing, or blood type; as such, generic eating programs need to be approached with caution.

I commenced writing ideas for this chapter on Day 3 of a self-imposed 7-day detoxification program - it had been a while since my last cleanse. I believe it is healthy, every now and then, to give my body a break from all the toxic food and beverages I may tend to ingest as part of daily or weekly habits. I undertook the detoxification under strict guidelines, to ensure that I thoroughly understood the process, and was well supported from a nutritional perspective.

Probably the most crucial point I would emphasise here is that, just like one specific healing modality may not provide a solution for everybody, no isolated eating plan or dietary program will necessarily result for everyone in noticeable weight reduction, improved energy or other desired results. We need to become aware of the language of our own body, and how to listen to its messages more effectively. Muscle testing is an incredibly useful tool, probably not as a means of self-diagnosis, but is certainly a reliable technique when undertaken by an experienced professional. It can even be used to determine food intolerances.

I have always been intrigued by the nature of allergies and why some people respond significantly to certain allergens while others seem to demonstrate little, if any, sensitivity. This would certainly indicate that, despite human beings sharing anatomical similarities with one another, we are all unique in how we present in the world, and we all process our environment in different ways. There are some other important considerations to note about maintaining optimal physical health (all of which is probably prior knowledge).

Maintaining a Healthy Biochemistry

When is the last time your general practitioner requested a blood test to measure your body chemistry? It is phenomenal the increasing number of people whose levels of magnesium, B vitamins and zinc are incredibly low, while similarly exhibiting above average quantities of heavy metal toxicity.

Being Conscious of what You Put on Your Body

I have been amazed in the past when I hear people talk about the importance of clean eating, only to discover that the same people use cosmetic and personal care products that are riddled with petrochemicals, sulphates, aluminium and other harsh synthetic and potentially carcinogenic ingredients. We need to make informed choices about what we put on our skin, as well as what we ingest, including the water we drink – water that is optimally alkalised is highly recommended.

Movement and Exercise

Gentle exercise is known to be beneficial, not only to maintain and improve physical fitness, but also to maximise the state of our mental health. If the body is not utilised in a way that promotes joint viscosity, muscle flexibility and strength, and optimal nerve conductivity, it may start to function less effectively, which may ultimately cause mental and emotional stress.

Activity 6: Connecting with Your Heart Centre, and Listening to the Subtle Language of the Body

I was first guided through this process after I had awoken one morning and was lying in bed just focusing on my breathing. My awareness was directed to my heart space, after which I experienced an amazing clarity, so much so that I had a profound vision that helped me to be more present in my own heart; I felt it could possibly facilitate others in the same way, and similarly could enable the development of further intuition regarding the physical body. You may choose to modify this to suit your own intuitive inclinations; whatever helps you to become more present and heart-centred is perfect.

The heart is the first organ to grow in the physical body, and I believe it is a magnificent source of energy, a logical starting point for connecting with the rest of the body. The objective of this activity is twofold: Firstly, to familiarise yourself with the practice of heart-centred presence; and, secondly to develop an intuitive connection with the language and messages of the physical body. It will help to find a quiet place, perhaps in nature or in a secluded part of your home, where you can meditate without any interference for about 10-15 minutes.

Close your eyes and be aware of your breathing. Gently inhale and exhale 3 times; as you do so, bring your attention to your body, particularly any places where you are experiencing discomfort, pain, inflammation or restlessness. Continue to breathe with ease, gently and consciously; with every breath you become more and more relaxed. You are now aware of the presence of a tubular ray of light extending from your soul star chakra, located approximately 30 centimetres above the top of your head, down to your heart chakra, located at the centre of your body.

Gently bring your inner visual awareness to the top of your head. I invite you to visualise your energetic consciousness travelling from the top of your head down through your skull into your physical brain. Allow yourself to visualise moving through your brain and see the structures that are held within the cranial area. Follow your visual journey down through the throat area, into the chest area. Really spend some time being present with, and connecting to, what you see and experience in your own anatomy. Continue into the physical heart, and perceive the four chambers; use your visual, auditory and intuitive senses to be fully present with the resonance of your heart.

Now gently shift your attention to a point approximately 2 centimetres (or 1 inch) behind the physical heart, just in front of the spine. Visualise a tiny speck of light, right there in the centre of your body. With every breath now, the tiny speck is becoming more and more intense, brighter and more vibrant. Continue to breathe gently, allowing this light to grow. It is now taking the form of a multi-faceted star and is expanding to the size of your physical heart.

You now see one of the facets, or points, break free from the star; this illuminated shard of bright light is now going to travel around your body in search of areas of stagnation, inflammation and darkness. With your intuition fully engaged, move your senses alongside the shard, which is like a fluorescent torch; travel with it down and up each of your upper limbs; then down towards your stomach and lower limbs. Explore every part of your body, particularly the places where you have noticed discomfort or irregularity. As you do so, take note of any feelings or insights that come to you in relation to your physical body.

When you have completed your illuminated search of your internal body, return with the shard back to your heart. The shard re-joins with the bright star behind your heart. This bright star is your own sacred heart. Allow it to expand even more, until its radiance covers your entire physical vessel and greater auric body. This light is the light of transcendence and transformation; your entire being is now immersed in its brilliance. This is the true power of your luminous heart, the Christ consciousness that lives inside you. Remain in this vibration for as long as you need. When you are ready, visualise the light retracting back to your centre; it is reducing more and more in size, until it once again returns to a speck of light behind your physical heart. Keep your awareness in your heart space as you continue to breathe into your centre. Become aware once again of the sounds and smells of the room; gently wriggle your fingers and toes, and when you feel ready, slowly open your eyes.

After this activity, you may like to spend some time reflecting on your experiences during the visualisation. Any feeling or observation you make, irrespective of how significant or otherwise you may think it is, write your reflections down; these reflections will be very informative as you proceed with this activity in the future. I would recommend repeating this meditation fortnightly, if not weekly, for whatever period it takes to connect freely with your heart centre and start experiencing intuitive insight.

Comments / Notes / Observations

SEAN C. SULLIVAN

CHAPTER 11

Conclusion

Looking behind, I am filled with gratitude;

Looking forward, I am filled with vision;

Looking upwards, I am filled with strength;

Looking within, I am filled with peace.

- Quero Apache Prayer

I t has no doubt become obvious by this stage that I am very passionate about two specific fields of interest: Firstly, the transformation in people from the debilitating state of suffering to the liberating energy of freedom; and secondly, the nature, quality and delivery of holistically meaningful and connected education programs. At the commencement of this journey, I highlighted the role that I believe stress plays in people's lives. The conclusion that was drawn, was that human beings in contemporary times are not biologically equipped to adequately process the growing severity and intensity of the stressful stimuli with which we are continually confronted. Allopathic medical strategies frequently involve the introduction of pharmaceutical interventions, often coupled with other psychological processes, to facilitate an improvement in symptoms attributed to high anxiety or extreme depressive tendencies. While such approaches may have short term benefits for a person's mental and emotional stability, they simply alleviate the symptoms, not the origin of imbalance.

We have explored a selection of key tools that, when combined and implemented as part of a daily conscious practise, have the potential to achieve lasting results in moving from a state of restlessness to a place of peace. Through sharing the wisdom teachings of some of my own life experiences, and including a selection of practical activities, I have attempted to demonstrate in a simple way the nature of energy and how we, individually, hold the keys to our own transformation.

In Chapter 3, we examined the way traumatic experiences and inherited belief systems can imbed themselves in our luminous matrix; the shamans of the Peruvian highlands have affirmed that such stagnant and misused energy can, and does, hijack the central nervous system, creating dis-ease in the physical body. We later explored how understanding the subtle communication system of the human body can invariably offer insight into illness and disease; unfortunately, human beings are similarly very skilled at disguising any malady that presents, often downplaying or ignoring physiological signs until pain and inflammation either abate, or present in an increasingly intense way that suddenly makes the situation very 'real'.

Further on, the notion of balance was discussed with reference to the constant exchange between our own sacred masculine and feminine energy, and the way in which the native Andean philosophy of *ayni*, impacts our relationship with everything in the universe. We similarly explored how we can bring a little more balance to our lives through the daily practice of meditation, and by inviting the healing power of music and sound into our environment.

The pivotal concept that I highlighted was in relation to the importance of tapping into the aspect of infinite possibility that resides within each of us, by allowing our unique creative expression to flow freely in and around us. If you can recall my earlier discussion regarding the upgrading of software, I made the comment that in order to make a transition from a restless state, it is necessary to upgrade to a new way of being.

The reflections I selected to incorporate in this book have unfolded over some 20 years of journeying. Along the way, I have experimented with many tools and processes, some successful and some not so, that have enabled me to, little by little, transform energy more effortlessly from a state of restlessness to a state of peace. Regardless of whether or not the activities and reflections resonate with you, I invite you unconditionally to be adventurous and courageous in your own path to self-mastery. In truth, it is every individual person's mission to discover the methods that resonate for them, that enable a transformation from the old restless consciousness to a new awakened way of being in the world.

Obstacles and challenges will always occur in life, as will triumphs and celebrations; that is the ebb and flow-like nature of the human experience. As humans, when we discover that sense of presence within, and are totally conscious in the moment, we come to understand the essence of who we are. Who *I* truly am is neither a culmination of what I have done, nor the myriad thought processes I filter, or the stories that I tell myself about myself. Who *I* am is not a concept that I can articulate with words. Who *I* am is an aspect of infinitely expanding consciousness.

Recall the metaphor I offered earlier about the leaf, and how it is a unique expression of a much greater whole. When we discover the connected consciousness that is already within each of us, we can begin to observe the profound connectedness we share with others and with everything that exists in the universe; and that realisation is the true expression of love. With practice of certain processes that refine the experience of living consciously, we can move closer to becoming present in every moment, and experience what spiritual masters describe as the ultimate union of doing and being.

SEAN C. SULLIVAN

I offer my sincere thanks and gratitude to you, the reader, for being present with me throughout this book. I wish you every success as you continue to explore and expand your awakening consciousness.

New Beginning

Awaken from this dream, my slate is clean.
At a second glance, another chance.
Forgiveness is the only key;
My thoughts have cleared, now I can see.

All at once I hear my name,
It's a conscious call to join the game.
All at once I feel alive and
I'm ready and willing to take a dive.

It's a new beginning, it's a time for change;
A time to feel the energy running through my veins.
No-one try to stop me, for I will plough straight through.
Who is in control of this life? Well, I guess it's up to you!

I am on my way now to bigger and better things.
I would fly away right now if I could grow wings.
I know my time is not complete, I'll have to wait and see;
Get on with life and realise that what will be, will be.

It's a new beginning, it's a time for change;
A time to feel the energy running through my veins.
No-one try to stop me, for I will plough straight through.
Who is in control of this life? Well, I guess it's up to you!

An amazing chapter is now coming to a close.
How will is conclude my friend? Nobody knows!
Stay in tune, stay on the track, there is no more to say.
Today was just a memory and tomorrow's a brand-new day.

It's a new beginning, it's a time for change;
A time to feel the energy running through my veins.
No-one try to stop me, for I will plough straight through.
Who is in control of this life? Well, I guess it's up to you!

- Original Lyrics by Sean C. Sullivan

Comments / Notes / Observations

_____

_____

_____

_____

_____

_____

_____

_____

_____

_____

_____

_____

_____

_____

Comments / Notes / Observations

_____

_____

_____

_____

_____

_____

_____

_____

_____

_____

_____

Comments / Notes / Observations

Acknowledgements

How does one succinctly describe the enormous contributions made by so many beautiful souls over a lifetime of learning? I send my love, thanks and gratitude wholeheartedly and unconditionally to my parents, family, friends, soul family, spiritual mentors and invisible guides - past, present and future - for the transformative gifts that have cumulatively enabled my personal and spiritual evolution, which have, in turn, culminated in the creation of this book.

There are so many people who have inspired and motivated my journey to this point; however, I would like to make mention of a few special people with whom connection through Spirit has been a source of great expansion and deep growth. To my dear friends Emerald, Siggi, Raghida, Leisa, Terry, Laura, Tim, Rania and Anna - *hatun munay* (great love) to you my brothers and sisters. To the spiritual avatars of our time whose discoveries and teachings have facilitated this process - thank you for your wisdom and invisible guidance.

To my partner in life, Rachael and our delightful children, Claire and Liam - words do not quite depict the nature of our connection; nor do they fully capture the powerful space we hold for one another. I am blessed to be walking alongside you all at this special time, and I look forward to the next exciting phase of the unfolding mystery of our shared life.

And finally, to the clients, workshop attendees, festival delegates, colleagues and audience members, either whom I have had the pleasure of meeting, or with whom I have yet to enjoy sharing consciousness: Thank you for your support both now and in the future. *Mahalo* (deep gratitude) to you, my brothers and sisters!

Sean C. Sullivan

SEAN C. SULLIVAN

About the Author

Sean C. Sullivan is a qualified educator, energy medicine practitioner, massage therapist, sound clinician, organic cosmetic artisan, loving husband and proud father of two. At the age of 17, a serious car accident directed Sean on a pathway of transformation, that would see him eventually undertake a guided spiritual journey, one that would be filled with self-discovery, reflection and healing.

After several years of soul-searching, formal studying and personal growth, in 2012 Sean embarked on the courageous journey from wounded healer to sage, known as the *Medicine Wheel*. Under the mentoring of highly-respected practitioners of the Inca shamanic lineage, Sean received initiations, wisdom teachings, and access to the sacred tools and practices of a spiritual tradition that has survived the ages.

As a full mesa carrier in the Inca shamanic tradition, Sean now blends his own intuitive messages from Source with the wisdom teachings of his Incan ancestors, alongside those of Traditional Chinese Medicine and Indigenous Australia. He has been described as a gifted teacher, and a compassionate healer, whose primary motivation is the spiritual evolution of the collective human consciousness.

Sean enjoys working in small and large group contexts, as well as with individual clients, and offers a wide range of workshop and retreat opportunities. Further information about upcoming events can be found at: www.trinitywellbeing.com.au .

SEAN C. SULLIVAN

www.ingramcontent.com/pod-product-compliance
Lightning Source LLC
LaVergne TN
LVHW021509080426
835509LV00018B/2460